Fact and Fiction: Literature across the Curriculum

Bernice E. Cullinan
Editor

International Reading Association
Newark, Delaware 19714, USA

The International Reading Association attempts, through its publications, to provide a forum for a wide spectrum of opinions on reading. This policy permits divergent viewpoints without assuming the endorsement of the Association.

Director of Publications   Joan M. Irwin
Managing Editor   Romayne McElhaney
Associate Editor   Anne Fullerton
Assistant Editor   Amy Trefsger
Editorial Assistant   Janet Parrack
Production Department Manager   Iona Sauscermen
Graphic Design Coordinator   Boni Nash
Design Consultant   Larry Husfelt
Desktop Publishing Supervisor   Wendy Mazur
Desktop Publishing   Anette Schuetz-Ruff
                        Cheryl Strum
                        Richard James
Proofing   Florence Pratt
              Toni Wright
Illustrations   Dave Bailey

Library of Congress Cataloging in Publication Data
Fact and fiction: literature across the curriculum/Bernice E. Cullinan, editor.
    p.   cm.
Includes bibliographical references and indexes.
1. Literature—Study and teaching (Elementary)—United States.
2. Interdisciplinary approach in education—United States. I. Cullinan, Bernice E.
LB1575.5.U5F33   1993   92-44494
372.64'044—dc20   CIP
ISBN 0-87207-380-7

Contents

Foreword

It is heartening to see the trend of including literature of fact and fiction in all subject areas of the school curriculum. For so long the curriculum was segmented and fractured, each subject assigned to an allotted number of minutes with no continuity among the topics. It was as if we envisioned the learner's brain as an old-fashioned card-catalog case with individual drawers to be opened and filled with information and then shut when another subject was pursued. Today educators are striving to approach learning as a whole, and literature is seen as an integral part of this whole.

Books of fact have for too long been seen as dry and only useful for research or reports. The label they are frequently given, "nonfiction," connotes that these books, being "not fiction," are less valued. As semantics *is* everything, I have been trying for several years to have people call books of fact by a more appropriate label—"informational books." This positive term denotes that the books provide the reader with information, but it also leads the reader to approach the books in a positive way and expect to receive from them more than facts for a report.

Indeed, good informational books are written with as much style and potency as the best of fiction. Their authors are intrigued by their subjects and write in such a way as to convey this to their readers. It is possible to locate informational books on almost any topic imaginable—science, social studies, math, health, language, and the arts all have been treated in good books. Educators and students can enhance the curriculum by seeking out the best informational books and incorporating them into the curriculum. And don't forget that informational books can be great read-alouds as well.

Another aspect of literature that must be an integral part of the whole curriculum is poetry. Too frequently poetry has been relegated to a brief study that dissects the structure and ignores the affective domain. As educators become more familiar with the range of poetry available, they will discover that there is a poem for almost any subject or mood. Poetry must be an everyday occurrence to have its full effect.

Fiction also has a place in a well-rounded curriculum. There are obvious ties—such as using historical fiction to bring a time period or event to life, or reading folklore to gain a sense of a culture. But there are other ways to use fiction to good advantage.

Many suggestions are given in this book to give you specific strategies and topics for instruction. The value of this book lies, however, in serving as a stimulus to get your own ideas flowing. Working cooperatively with colleagues at your grade level or in your content area will yield a wealth of ways for you to incorporate books of fact and fiction in your total curriculum.

M. Jean Greenlaw
University of North Texas

Contributors

Richard F. Abrahamson
University of Houston
Houston, Texas

Adela Artola Allen
University of Arizona
Tucson, Arizona

Betty Carter
Texas Woman's University
Denton, Texas

Diana Cohn
Little Red Schoolhouse
New York, New York

Bernice E. Cullinan
New York University
New York, New York

James Flood
San Diego State University
San Diego, California

Diane Lapp
San Diego State University
San Diego, California

Linda S. Levstik
University of Kentucky
Lexington, Kentucky

Sara J. Wendt
Little Red Schoolhouse
New York, New York

Introduction

Bernice E. Cullinan

A virtual explosion is occurring in the book world: Thousands more outstanding trade books for children are rolling off printing presses with each publishing season. New publishing companies, new divisions within companies, and increased production in established companies contribute to the tremendous volume of fact and fiction books now available for young readers. The boom in children's books is undoubtedly the major publishing trend of the late 20th century.

This explosion of children's books has many positive implications for elementary and middle school educators and particularly for teachers who want to use high-quality literature across the curriculum. But, in the tradition of the chicken-and-egg puzzle, it must be noted that educators are at least partly responsible for the explosion: For many reasons and for many years, they have been calling for increased use of trade books in the classroom. Teachers and librarians have long observed that students learn best when they

- are personally involved with the material they read,
- become engaged in a topic, and
- have a context and framework for understanding facts.

These conditions prevail when children read trade books.

Teachers and librarians also know that students want to read material that is interesting and engaging, focuses on a specific topic in depth, and presents a new point of view. A trade book presents its author's personal view on a topic, his or her way of seeing and interpreting information. Textbooks serve different purposes: conveying facts, presenting summaries, introducing topics, or providing instructions for activities or questions for assessment, for example. Even well written textbooks, however, cover sweeping generations of history or provide information on a vast number of topics; less well written ones contain sweeping generalizations presented from a single point of view or are nothing more than a dry collection of facts. Clearly one such book per subject area cannot serve the needs and interests of the broad range of students in today's classrooms.

As society becomes more diverse, student populations become more diverse. A single point of view is simply no longer adequate. Students want books that acknowledge their cultural group and depict people like themselves; they want books that link the information presented to real life and make the subject matter interesting and relevant. When it comes to teaching today's students, we need to provide depth as well as breadth. No single book—no matter how good—can do this.

One way to meet the demands of teaching diverse content to diverse students is to use multiple texts written by authors who care deeply and know a great deal about their subject. We have more good books on more diverse topics than we have ever had before; this makes it possible to develop programs that use literature across the curriculum. If, for example, you want to use a novel to enliven a study of the American Civil War, you can choose from at least 15 good ones. If you want to teach about the sea creatures that live in tidal pools, you can choose from 10 excellent informational books. If you want to read about dinosaurs, you can select from more than 50 books.

The authors who have contributed to *Fact and Fiction* demonstrate how we can choose wisely from the wealth of books available. They also show us how to use the books in many areas of the curriculum. Linda Levstik leads off by demonstrating how historical fiction makes the past come to life. She shows us that these novels personalize historical events and periods and help readers see history as human experience.

Adela Artola Allen reminds us that the world is made up of people from many cultures and that the books we use need to reflect those cultures. The world is not a melting pot but, to use a metaphor Allen relates, an orchestra in which cultures and countries are the instruments that can blend to create wonderful music. Betty Carter and Richard Abrahamson introduce nonfiction as the primary learning material across diverse curriculum areas within the social studies. They demonstrate that the days of dull nonfiction are gone, and that there is a new wealth of informational books available to interest and delight children. They also show how young readers build literary ladders of understanding by moving from fiction to nonfiction and back to fiction as they explore topics in the social studies.

Diana Cohn and Sara Wendt demonstrate vividly how they use literature to develop concepts in math class. They draw from their colleagues to present titles appropriate for a broad age range and describe numerous activities for learning about money, time, classification, and arithmetic.

Finally, Diane Lapp and James Flood show how trade books can supplement textbooks to help students understand science concepts. They compare the way topics are treated in both types of books and show how students respond to the different texts. Their idea of a "complementary curriculum" has implications for teachers who want to use both textbooks and trade books in any subject area.

Although each author in this volume focuses on a specific area, all show how the areas complement and support one another and how literature helps in this process. Together these chapters will inspire you to explore trade books in new ways and to work toward an integrated curriculum in which outstanding literature is the heart.

Chapter 1

Making the Past Come to Life

Linda S. Levstik

In a fifth grade classroom, a young girl tries to make sense of the contradictory perspectives about the American Revolution presented in the historical novels and the textbook passages she has read. She wonders why her social studies text "just says that the Americans were right but it doesn't tell you exactly why they were right, or why the British fought," while the trade books (the historical novels) led her to believe that things "weren't too great for either side.... How could the rebels and loyalists do such stupid things and all the social studies books leave out anything bad that the Americans did, and it's always the British?"

In another classroom, a second grade teacher reads aloud Ann Grifalconi's *The Village of Round and Square Houses*. Soon, a round house made of paper and straw turns the classroom's reading center into a piece of rural Cameroon. A guest originally from Cameroon visits to teach the children songs and dances and to tell stories from her country's history. Later the children use nonfiction trade books and reference texts to help them create a mural of urban Cameroon's high-rise buildings and busy streets. Their teacher points out that the round and square houses of rural Cameroon are a bit like the log cabins that used to dot the rural parts of their own state. "Things change over time," she tells her students, "and all that is how we come to have history."

Rather than relying on the often lackluster material that appears in so many history textbooks, the children in both of these classrooms encounter history in a form that sparks their interest and encourages their imagination. In the first case, historical fiction raises questions about justice, morality, historical perspective, and the accuracy of the information presented in textbooks; in the second case, fiction and informational books are used to make connections between the past and present of two cultures. A growing body of research suggests that historical literature can influence students' imaginative entry into the past (see, for example, Egan, 1983; Levstik, 1986, 1990a; Meek, Warlow, & Barton, 1978). Unlike textbooks, trade books—and particularly historical fiction—personalize history, explore human experience, embed historical information in a context of cause and effect, and provide a framework for interpreting historical information (Downey & Levstik, 1991; Levstik, 1990a).

Personalizing History

Textbooks often strive to present as many objectively documented facts as possible and thereby lose the life of the past in a proliferation of detail. Historical fiction, on the other hand, thrives on life. These books give meaning to historical events by presenting them in a social context and subjecting them to that society's morality (White, 1980, pp. 14-18). This is very appealing to children. Consider, for instance, one fifth grader's comments:

> The social studies book is old and doesn't have as much information in it like books do—they give you a lot of information that no social studies book ever tells you.... The social studies book doesn't give you a lot of detail. You don't imagine yourself there because they're not doing it as if it were a person. That would be a very interesting social studies book if they

told a few things about the people as if it were from their own eyes. But textbooks don't like to be interesting especially.

As this child points out, textbooks do not view history personally. Rather, they eliminate humanizing details in favor of broad coverage and often sweeping generalizations: not *this* person facing *this* situation, but faceless masses, unconnected to human joys and fears and untouched by doubts, bravery, or cowardice, engaging in some dryly presented event. Historical fiction, on the other hand, invites the reader to enter into a historical discussion that involves asking questions and making judgments. What was it like to be a person here? What was the nature of morality in this particular time and place? With whom shall my sympathies lie?

Of course, some historical novels raise more penetrating questions than others. Some writers choose to present only one point of view or interpretation of a historical event, perhaps because they feel there *is* only one legitimate point of view or because they believe young readers are unable to cope with conflicting viewpoints. These writers' stories are painted in black and white with few touches of gray. Esther Forbes's *Johnny Tremain*, for instance, is a well-written story set during the American Revolution but it does not give the reader an opportunity to enter the heart or mind of, say, a sympathetic loyalist wrestling with the moral dilemmas posed by holding unpopular opinions during a revolutionary period. As Taxel (1978) points out, such books may serve to reinforce simplistic images of historical events and eras and leave out significant portions of society—especially the poor, working classes, women, and minorities (p. 8).

Later historical fiction (*Johnny Tremain* was published in 1943) is more likely to challenge readers to make hard choices along with literary characters. In Christopher and James Lincoln Collier's *My Brother Sam Is Dead*, the agony of unclear choices and the insanity of war are seen through the eyes of a character torn between a loyalist father and a rebel brother. Avi's *The True Confessions of Charlotte Doyle* deals with the power of social and economic class to blind us to evil and the power of sexism to blind us to ability. Katherine Paterson's *Lyddie* invites readers to consider some of the forms oppression can take, from slavery to economic bondage in an industrial society. In books such as these, powerful themes are presented through the eyes of individuals who communicate the personal, emotional, and psychological impact of living in and through historical eras and events.

Exploring Human Experience

Historical literature provides a context for children to explore human experiences and human nature. Elementary students report being moved, inspired, and sometimes angered by what they read in historical fiction, and add often that they learned something they labeled "the truth" from these books; the frequency with which these children describe a "need to know" about various topics in history is remarkable (Levstik, 1986, 1990a, 1990b).

Reading and discussing both historical fiction and nonfiction appears to help children explore both the worst and the best of human behavior and test their own potential for good or evil. In one study, children wondered aloud about what they would have done in particular situations: "Why didn't they run away? I would have!" declared a sixth grader after reading some selections of holocaust literature (Levstik, 1986). In another study, a first grade boy identified with Columbus: "I was Columbus, and I saw the night sky and the moon. And I saw the stars come together and make things" (Levstik, 1990a).

These readers were not looking for historical information in the traditional sense. Rather, they were seeking emotional truth and an understanding of how past human experience might affect their lives. As one child said about a work of historical fiction, "I loved this book because it sees through the eyes of this person. I never knew how hard people had it. This book is so real. I find this period especially interesting for some reason I don't know about" (Levstik, 1986).

Probing Cause and Effect

The structure of historical fiction can influence the way in which history is perceived. These books are usually organized in a cause-and-effect structure. In one sense, then, historical fiction forces history to conform to certain narrative norms, to have a beginning point and a place where matters are resolved. The flow of narrative links action with reaction in a powerful emotional context, so that readers come to feel as well as know about historical events and to place these events within the continuum of history. In social studies textbooks, historical events often are presented as if they were unrelated to other historical events—one chapter may relate the "facts" of the Crusades, for example, and another may move on to a discussion of the Protestant Reformation, without much indication of how the two may be connected or placed within the continuum of history. And these textbooks usually omit entirely any mention of how historical events have relevance in modern life and what they may reveal about human nature. The narrative structure of historical fiction, on the other hand, tends to carry readers along and involve them in the cause-and-effect lessons that history offers to modern society. Thus, readers of Mildred Taylor's *Roll of Thunder, Hear My Cry*, a story of the American civil rights era, begin to understand the kind of courage it takes to face virulent racism and to relate the events depicted to race relations in the past and in the present. Both Bette Bao Lord's *In the Year of the Boar and Jackie Robinson* and Sollace Hotze's *A Circle Unbroken* raise issues of clashes between cultures and may help children understand the role that intolerance of cultural differences has played throughout human history.

The cause-and-effect structure in historical fiction most often involves motivation. Why do characters behave in particular ways? What motivates their choices? When Meribah Simons in Kathryn Lasky's *Beyond the Divide* is abandoned in rugged mountains with a disabled wagon, readers know the character of each member of the deserting party and the events that stripped them of even a veneer of civilization. Readers also know Meribah's strength and her will to survive. There is more information about what happened to people who journeyed west in this scene than could ever be found in a textbook. This sort of powerful depiction of motivation reveals fundamental truths about the human condition and helps children understand both the events of the past and themselves.

Interpreting the Past

Historical literature provides a window through which children can interpret the past. Learning about history can be a lively process of selecting, organizing, interpreting, and reinterpreting data. Knowing the date of the Battle of Hastings, for instance, is irrelevant if one has no framework in which to interpret that fact. Interpretation, in broad terms, has a significant impact on how we understand historical events. Every time children learn that

Columbus "discovered" America, for example, they learn an interpretation of history. It is important that children be made aware that a variety of interpretations—some of which may be more legitimate than others—exists. How might Columbus' voyage to the Americas be interpreted by a Native American historian? Or how might those tried, convicted, and executed in the Salem witch trials interpret the history of religious freedom in New England?

One fifth grader, after comparing her textbook with what she had learned by reading historical fiction, declared that she would never have lived in Massachusetts during the early colonial period: "They didn't have religious freedom! They were stupid and killed people for their beliefs. I'd go maybe to Pennsylvania. It was more free there, I think." This child was involved in interpreting history. She used facts and feelings to order the past in a meaningful way and challenged the interpretation of history presented in her textbook. Literature fed her need to understand the past and helped her learn that there is more than one way of looking at things.

Teaching the Past

As teachers we should work to feed children's hunger to understand the past. Using literature in the classroom is not the only way to do that, but it can be a powerful component of a good elementary social studies program. Teachers must, however, consider the literary and historical merit of the literature they use as well as the potential of particular books to support in-depth historical inquiry. The power of a literary interpretation of history places a burden on the classroom teacher to select the finest books available for children. A good story does not compensate for bad history, nor does good history justify a poorly written text. In selecting literature to support historical study, teachers and librarians should ask themselves the following questions.

Do illustrations and text work together? An increasing number of picture books and storybooks for young children have historical themes or settings. In such books, text and illustrations should work together to tell the story. Often the illustrations provide information not explicitly mentioned in the text. For instance, in George Ella Lyon's *Cecil's Story* it is only Peter Catalanotto's illustrations that place the story in the American Civil War. A young boy's father has gone off to war, and may not come home.

The text describes the boy's desire to take care of his father's work at home—chop wood and feed the pigs and chickens. But how can he guide the mule and plow through the fields when he isn't as high as the plow's handles? The artist interprets the child's fears in a series of delicate and moving illustrations that link the reader to a particular historical time as well as to universal feelings.

Does the author use the language well? Lyon, for instance, uses a spare but elegant vocabulary that fits both the story and the period in *Cecil's Story*. Pam Conrad's language resonates with the power and intensity of life on the prairie in *Prairie Songs*. She frames her story with an evocative description of the prairie in the opening paragraph and a peaceful scene of community life in the final stages.

Is the story clichéd? Some historical literature tends toward saccharine nostalgia, more suited to adult sentimentality than to either historical reality or children's interests. The best historical fiction for children offers young readers fresh insights into human experience. When the main character in Katherine Paterson's *Lyddie* decides to enter Oberlin College rather than to accept a marriage proposal, readers are invited to rethink the romantic conclusion that used to be considered the only possible "happy ending." One fifth grader put down Sollace Hotze's *A Circle Unbroken* and said, "I never thought that someone would want to go back to the Indians, that they would feel Indian even though they looked white—and that's the ending you want, for her to go home to the Indians." A third grader read the end of Ann Turner's *Nettie's Trip South* and pondered the effect of having only one name, and that one thrust upon you by someone else. Books such as these give children the opportunity to experience outstanding literature while experiencing history.

Is the text historically accurate? Too often historical accuracy is ignored if a book's language is beautiful and its illustrations are striking. If literature is to be used to spur historical understanding, however, content is as crucial as literary merit. In Robert Newton Peck's popular *A Day No Pigs Would Die*, for instance, an otherwise interesting story is inaccurate in its depiction of the Shakers. Members of this virtually extinct sect, who practiced celibacy and lived communally, are presented in Peck's story as living in traditional, nuclear families. An author who includes historical content in a published work has an obligation to present information that is as accurate as possible. Young readers will often accept historical information if it is embedded in a captivating text, even when presented with contrary information in a textbook (Levstik, 1990a). It is only with direct teacher intervention that misinformation is dislodged and students become critical readers of historical literature.

What historical interpretation is developed in the text? As has been noted, interpretations of historical events vary. Literature can help focus children's attention on the issue of interpretation. Why, for instance, might an author want to tell a story in a particular way? One second grade teacher uses Eve Bunting's *How Many Days to America? A Thanksgiving Story* to lead children into a discussion about Thanksgiving in the context of immigrants coming to America. She asks children to imagine why the author wrote this book. What did she want her readers to understand? The children generally decide that Bunting wanted to talk about welcoming new immigrants and being thankful for their safe arrival. Another teacher uses Russell Freedman's *Immigrant Kids* and Riki Levinson's *Watch the Stars Come Out* to show how two authors can use the same sources and still interpret the immigrant experience quite differently.

Children need to engage in these sorts of discussions that lead them to be sensitive to the interpretive nature of historical fiction. They need to be exposed not just to textbooks and historical fiction, but also to biographies, autobiographies, informational texts, and even oral history; they need to be able to distinguish the features of each form and to recognize their strengths and limitations. They will then learn to ask who is telling the story and to whom, and who is left out. Do all the stories of the American Revolution, for instance, promote the idea that the British were awful and the Americans clearly in the right? Is settlement of the "New World" always presented as an unmitigated good, without attention being paid to its impact on native peoples? Or, on the other hand, are native people presented as being exclusively in the right and all settlers portrayed as ravagers of the land? Is history always *his* story and never *her* story?

No single book can handle all possible points of view. Teachers must seek out a variety of materials to provide a balance. A good social studies program should provide alternative viewpoints using textbooks, role-playing, films, and guest speakers, in addition to numerous selections of literature. In this way, literature becomes one component of a program of systematic inquiry into powerful themes that actively engage children in researching, reading, writing, discussing, and sharing what they learn.

References

Downey, M., & Levstik, L.S. (1991). Teaching and learning history. In J. Shaver (Ed.), *Handbook of research on social studies*. New York: Macmillan.

Egan, K. (1983). Accumulating history. *History and theory: Studies in the philosophy of history* (pp. 66-80). Belkeft 22. Middletown, CT: Wesleyan University Press.

Levstik, L.S. (1986). The relationship between historical response and narrative in a sixth-grade classroom. *Theory and Research in Social Education, 14,* 1-15.

Levstik, L.S. (1990a). *I prefer success: Subject specificity in a first grade setting.* Paper presented at the meting of the American Educational Research Association, Boston, MA.

Levstik, L.S. (1990b). Research directions: Mediating content through literary texts. *Language Arts, 67*(8), 848-853.

Meek, M., Warlow, A., & Barton, G. (1978). Introduction. In M. Meek, A. Warlow, & G. Barton (Eds.), *The cool web.* New York: Atheneum.

Taxel, J. (1978). The American revolution in children's books: Issues of racism and classism. *Bulletin of the Council on Interracial Books for Children, 12,* 7-8.

White, H. (1980). The value of narrativity in the representation of reality. *Critical Inquiry, 7*(1), 5-27.

Children's Books

Avi. (1990). *The true confessions of Charlotte Doyle.* New York: Orchard.

Bunting, E. (1988). *How many days to America? A Thanksgiving story.* New York: Clarion.

Collier, C., & Collier, J. (1974). *My brother Sam is dead.* New York: Four Winds.

Conrad, P. (1985). *Prairie songs.* New York: HarperCollins.

Forbes, E. (1943, reissued 1987). *Johnny Tremain.* Boston, MA: Houghton Mifflin.

Freedman, R. (1980). *Immigrant kids.* New York: Dutton.

Grifalconi, A. (1986). *The village of round and square houses.* Boston, MA: Little, Brown.

Hotze, S. (1988). *A circle unbroken.* New York: Clarion.

Lasky, K. (1983). *Beyond the divide.* New York: Macmillan.

Levinson, R. (1985). *Watch the stars come out.* New York: Dutton.

Lord, B.B. (1984). *In the year of the boar and Jackie Robinson.* New York: HarperCollins.

Lyon, G.E. (1991). *Cecil's story.* New York: Orchard.

Paterson, K. (1991). *Lyddie.* New York: Lodestar/Dutton.

Peck, R.N. (1972). *A day no pigs would die.* New York: Knopf.

Taylor, M. (1976). *Roll of thunder, hear my cry.* New York: Dial.

Turner, A. (1987). *Nettie's trip south.* New York: Macmillan.

Chapter 2

Diversity Education

Adela Artola Allen

C hildren today have access to world events at their fingertips through telecommunications. This exposure to happenings around the globe can be mirrored in a school curriculum that challenges students to seek a broad knowledge of the world's community of people. Through a deep multicultural understanding, children can be prepared to live in concert with their next-door neighbors and their neighbors around the world. They learn that people are interdependent and realize that we must take responsibility for the planet we all share.

The opportunity to help children develop a global view— one in which cultural diversity is celebrated—is ready-made in the multicultural environment of many classrooms. By the year 2000, one of three children in school in the United States, for example, will come from a nonmajority ethnic group. Greater numbers of children from Hispanic, African-American, Asian, Pacific Island, and Native-American families will be the classmates of children from white, European backgrounds. This diverse group of students will be the consumers of education and educational materials; they will be the future decision-makers and voters.

Such demographic changes, along with numerous incidents of racial unrest around the world, clearly indicate the need for radical change in education. Schools are an excellent place for combatting the prejudices and stereotypes that divide us; and education grounded in diversity is our most promising weapon. By celebrating differences among people in the classroom, encouraging respect for those differences, and recognizing all cultures' unique contributions, students are put on the path to becoming tolerant and compassionate world citizens.

Diversity education views "all cultures as coexistent and equally valid, abandoning paradigms that speak of cultures as 'underdeveloped,' 'overdeveloped,' and 'primitive.' It discards educational labels that describe non-white, non-middle-class students as 'culturally deprived,' 'disadvantaged,' or 'culturally deficient'" (García, 1982, p. 11). García draws an analogy between today's multicultural society and an orchestra and equates instrument groups with distinct cultures: "In an orchestra, each instrument belongs to a group that retains its identity; each group is interdependent with other instrument groups, and each instrument group contributes to the overall orchestral harmony" (p. 42).

When children feel secure in their own culture and are encouraged to explore their similarities and differences with people from other cultures—and ultimately to think critically about our common human condition—they are able to shed the limitations of an ethnocentric world view and exchange it for a global perspective. Evans (1987) reports that elementary students who attend classes where social studies programs focus on diversity education develop a more positive attitude toward themselves and people from other countries. Students also found more similarities than differences between themselves and others. In addition, Evans' findings show that children can think globally at a young age.

To accomplish its goals, diversity education requires two things: (1) educators' commitment to reflect on their values and beliefs with a pledge to adopt a global point of view, and (2) a commitment to infuse every strand of the curriculum with multicultural materials—especially literature—that celebrates all the world's peoples. The first requirement takes courage; the second takes time. The exciting rewards of diversity education for teachers, students, and communities, however, are well worth the effort.

The Harmonious Multicultural Classroom

Everyone inherits a culture; some of us inherit more than one. When we're very young we aren't really aware of our cultural heritage. We do not know, for instance, that being African-American is any different from being Vietnamese until we are confronted with the Vietnamese culture and gain some experience of Vietnamese impressions, behaviors, history, or actions that are different from our own. Confronting differences can be startling, and individual reactions can take many forms. Children with limited experience of cultures different from their own (monocultural children) are often apprehensive and unable to accept others whom they perceive as different from themselves. In the early grades, many children are confronted with members of other ethnic groups for the first time. For these children, "different" can mean "inferior." Early negative reactions to children of other cultures can be the beginning of prejudice. On the other hand, researchers in multicultural education report that children who have extensive exposure to more than one culture usually accommodate differences or shift from one culture to another to fit the social situation in which they find themselves.

Teachers as well as students can be monocultural and possibly unable to deal with students from cultures other than their own. They exhibit their discomfort by avoiding calling on these students, expecting the same participation in oral discussion from them as they do from mainstream students regardless of language abilities, singling them out as token representatives of their culture, or unwittingly making them feel inferior. Teachers who recognize and move away from their own monocultural attitudes and actions are taking the first step toward achieving the goals of diversity education.

The next step is to gather materials. When analyzing published educational materials, educators must realize that they largely favor concepts, experiences, and perspectives of the historic majority culture. In the United States, for example, there is little beyond token representation of nonwhite populations in much of the material offered to students. Although efforts have been made to incorporate multiethnic literature in some whole language programs and literature-based curricula, we still have a long way to go in providing students with materials that reflect the pluralism of modern society.

This situation creates an inhospitable educational environment for all children. Nonwhite children in North American schools can have problems of self-esteem because they don't find their cultural heritage valued in learning materials. Seeing themselves portrayed in print would contribute to these children's self-acceptance and demonstrate society's acknowledgment of their culture's contributions. It would also challenge white students' ethnocentricity, providing them with a richness of experience while expanding their perspective.

The importance of literature in diversity education cannot be overemphasized. Imparting new information within the structure of a story is an ideal method for teaching in many areas of a multicultural curriculum. "Children need the bridge that stories provide in order to link their growing understanding of other cultures to their personal experience and background knowledge" (Diakiw, 1990). We must exercise care in all book selection, however, and in multiethnic book selection in particular. Authors of children's books and the teachers who use these books in their classrooms must realize that children are susceptible to the power of stories. The view of the world presented in stories contributes to a child's developing worldview. The value of diversity must be clearly communicated in the materials we select.

Multicultural Materials: A Few Suggestions

Teachers pursuing diversity education should fill their classrooms with multiethnic materials collected with the help of students, parents, the school librarian or media specialist, and other teachers. A large world map, displayed prominently on a bulletin board, is an excellent focal point for the classroom. This map will be used in lessons throughout the year. Early in the school year, teachers can lead students in a discussion of the relationship of their home country to the rest of the countries depicted on the map. Students can be asked to find their families' countries of origin, perhaps marking them off with flag pins.

Native lands of authors, scientists, mathematicians, political figures, and so on can be flagged as their contributions are discussed in content area lessons. Students can be encouraged to share newspaper articles on countries of interest to them and find those countries on the map. Manila folders for each country studied can be kept near the map for filing clippings for future reference for writing activities or content area study. Interesting facts about a country's art, history, and discoveries, for example, can be added to the file by students, teachers, and guests. Throughout the year the map serves as a reminder of the connections among people, communities, and countries and demonstrates how interrelated we all are.

Teachers also need to gather a variety of print materials to expand on activities related to the classroom map. *The Macmillan Book of Fascinating Facts* by Ann Elwood and Carol Madigan is an excellent resource for expanding on beginning map activities and providing information for writing. American teachers find that Chapter 2, "The United States and the Old Country," answers many questions students have about their ancestors. Chapter 5, "Words and Language," is useful for activities related to language usage and can inspire students to compare folk wisdom revealed in proverbs from different cultures. (*Mexican-American Folklore* by John West and *The Diane Goode Book of American Folk Tales and Songs* compiled by Ann Durell are two other sources of folk wisdom.)

Articles found in periodicals such as *National Geographic, Smithsonian, Time, Condé Nast's Traveler, Americas, Archaeology,* and *Life* provide material to add to country folders or pictures for bulletin board displays. Used-book stores and garage sales offer these items at minimal prices. Newspaper clippings, photographs, postcards, and airline or travel agency magazines and brochures are valuable additions.

Informational books on multicultural topics can be kept in the classroom library. For primary grades, the Visual Geography series (Lerner Publications) offers excellent photographs that introduce the people, history, government, and geography of many nations. The World's Children series (Carolrhoda Books) provides an impressive visual experience of China, Egypt, Nepal, and Peru while introducing young readers to the daily life, history, and geography of these countries. The Ancient World series (Silver Burdett) focuses on family and community life, religion, form of government, and art of 13 ancient civilizations and is appropriate for upper-grade classrooms. Discussing the events that contributed to the rise and fall of each can provide a forum for critical thinking. The glossaries and timelines in each volume are exceptionally valuable.

There are many books available on specific cultures. For example, an upper-grade child might want to become an expert on Egypt. After reading Pamela Odijk's *The Egyptians* from the Ancient World series, he or she may consult *Egypt in Pictures, The Egyptian Word* (Margaret Oliphant), *Feats and Wisdom of the Ancients* (Time-Life Books Staff), and *Mummies, Masks, and Mourners* (Margaret Berrill). Berrill's book, part of the Time Detective Series, explores funeral rites around the world. Comparing spiritual beliefs and burial rituals will prompt further reading on related subjects. Paul Goble's *Beyond the Ridge*, for example, deals with Pueblo Indian spiritual beliefs and burial customs, Eve Bunting's *The Happy Funeral* depicts traditional ceremonies surrounding death, and Miska Miles's *Annie and the Old One* shows a grandmother teaching her granddaughter about death. Students can write in journals or participate in small-group discussions to share their feelings about what they've learned from reading about a different culture.

Milton Meltzer's books are invaluable for upper-grade students in a diversity education classroom. Meltzer takes the reader to the heart of the human experiences that create history. Particularly noteworthy are *The American Promise, Never to Forget: The Jews of the Holocaust, Rescue: The Story of How Gentiles Saved Jews in the Holocaust, The Jewish Americans: A History in Their Own Words, The Black Americans: A History in Their Own Words, The Hispanic Americans*, and *The Chinese Americans.*

After studying one culture, students might enjoy comparing cultures. Arts and crafts often make distinct cultural contributions. *23 Varieties of Ethnic Art and How to Make Each One* by Jean and Cle Kinney pays homage to the contributions to art of various ethnic groups in the United States. Using illustrated literature books is an excellent way to study a culture's art. *The Flame of Peace: A Tale of the Aztecs* (Deborah Nourse Lattimore) is lavishly decorated with symbols of this ancient culture. Leo and Diane Dillon's illustrations in *Ashanti to Zulu: African Traditions*

(Margaret Musgrove) portray details of cultures and capture the spirit of African art. *The Paper Crane* (Molly Bang) for younger students and *Sadako and the Thousand Paper Cranes* (Eleanor Coerr) for older students will spark interest in the Japanese art of origami.

Biographies of people who have excelled in their fields provide another means of incorporating diversity education in the curriculum. *The Ethnic Almanac* (S. Bernardo), *The Negro Almanac: A Reference Work on the Afro American* (Harry Ploski and James Williams), *Who's Who Among Hispanic Americans* (Amy Unterburger and Jane Delgado), and *Peoples of the World: Latin Americans* (Joyce Moss and George Wilson) are excellent general references in this area. Students might enjoy the easy-to-read *Famous Mexican Americans* by Janet Morey and Wendy Dunn with its biographies of ten contemporary Hispanic Americans. Sharing these biographies could lead to an animated discussion of human experiences, including the way these people overcame similar difficulties on their road to success. Individual's biographies, such as A.D. Porter's *Jump at the Sun: The Story of Zora Neale Hurston* or *César Chávez: Man of Courage* by F.M. White are also appropriate.

Although *Peak Performance: Sports, Science, and the Body in Action* by Emily Isberg is not a biography, it includes information about gymnast Siri Larsen, a Cambodian living in the U.S., and Kanellos Kanellopolous, a Greek national cycling champion, among others. Reading about international athletes leads to a discussion of the Olympics, an exciting topic for intermediate students that reflects the ideals of diversity education.

Expanding Understanding

General reading about different cultures leads naturally into more specific inquiry. It is a short leap for students to move from considering countries separately to thinking in terms of global cultural diversity. A good way to help this process along is to show students how practices in one culture relate to those in another. In all cultures, daily lives are governed by ritual: what we wear and why, what we eat and how we cook, how we play, how we celebrate, and so forth. Closely related to these day-to-day activities, and sometimes indistinguishable from them, are the sequences that people from different cultures use to order their activities and, ultimately, their worldview. Sequences such as the alphabet, days of the week, months of the year, ordinal and cardinal numbers, and holidays give order to a culture; without them, the activities that define a community or culture would be impossible.

Cultural sequences and rituals are determined by each culture's unique history and geography. Some cultural sequences are governed by science and immediately demonstrate to children the similarities that bond diverse peoples. For example, the Aztec calendar coincides almost exactly with our Gregorian calendar and is based on astronomical understanding of the solar year. Surprisingly—and often inexplicably—traditions, legends, and religious beliefs present many intercultural similarities, even when no known connection exists between cultures. An unexplained phenomenon such as the similarities in architecture, art, and hieroglyphics of the Mayans and the ancient Egyptians illustrates this. Regardless of the similarities, there is no known historical link between these two civilizations. Both the diversity and the similarity of rituals and cultural sequences serve as a scaffold on which an understanding of the common bonds between people can be built. Using this approach across the curriculum and at every grade level indelibly imprints global-thinking in the minds of students.

In elementary school, children delight in memorizing cultural sequences such as the alphabet and the days of the week. Learning sequences in other languages and discovering similarities and differences among languages is a fascinating challenge for these youngsters. Unearthing that Friday in English is *viernes* in Spanish and *vendredi* in French, and that this day was named in honor of the Norse goddess Frigg (in English) and the Roman goddess Venus (in Spanish and French) is delightful!

Children acquiring English will be enchanted to learn number sequence rhymes such as "One, two, buckle my shoe," and those learning Spanish will enjoy "*A la una como tuna, a las dos me de la tos, a las tres veo a Andres....*" *Ten, Nine, Eight* by Molly Bang offers a rhyme and a tender story for counting down to bedtime. "Cho—co—la—te," the finger counting Spanish counterpart to "This little pig went to market," can be found in *Tortillitas Para Mamá* (Margaret C. Griego). The Count Your Way Through series from Carolrhoda Books introduces readers to the numbers one through ten in the national language of a country and acquaints children with aspects of the culture, history, geography, and traditions of this country. Although phonetic transcriptions for the pronunciation of the numbers are provided, I suggest teachers try to locate native speakers and ask them to make a tape recording or visit the classroom to share their knowledge of a particular country while teaching the students to count. Students can work in groups to prepare questions for the speaker's visit. Upper-elementary students can research number systems of other cultures and ancient civilizations. The Roman and Arabic systems can be easily compared, for example.

The Aztec calendar and how it can be deciphered presents another topic for investigation by upper-elementary students. In one classroom, students drew the glyphs for the 20 day signs of the Aztec month and displayed them on the bulletin board. Another group wrote explanations of how the Aztec calendar of 360 plus 5 sacred days was organized. A third group researched and wrote a report on the sacred 260-day calendar used in Aztec religious rituals. Working out how the 20 signs matched with the numbers 1 to 13 to create 20 sets of 12 days resulted in a challenging multicultural extension into mathematics. In this classroom, *The Aztecs* by Frances Berdan was a valuable source of information for students. The book contains excellent pictures, a list of the names of all the native groups of North America, a bibliography, and a glossary. Brian Fagan's *The Aztecs* traces the Aztec society, philosophy, customs, ceremonies, and rise and collapse in a comprehensive resource for older children.

Many rituals revolve around eating—something people from all cultures do. For beginning readers, *Bread* by Dorothy Turner is an appropriate introduction to the subject of food from different cultures. This book looks at the history and production of bread, pointing out the regional and cultural differences and similarities of this universal staple. *Bread, Bread, Bread* by Ann Morris, an excellent book for all elementary students, explores the preparation and enjoyment of bread, its sale and distribution, and the rituals that surround bread making and eating in many cultures. Both of these books could trigger enjoyable projects such as baking bread in class or sampling different kinds of bread children bring to school from home.

Intermediate students may undertake a research project to discover the origin of popular foods such as noodles, corn, pumpkin pie, peppers, tortilla chips, hot dogs, pastrami, or tea. For example, children could begin by reading Aliki's *Corn Is Maize: The Gift of the Indians*. From this book, they learn how corn was discovered and used by Native Americans. In Leo Politi's *Three Stalks of Corn*, a story for young children, Angelica's grandmother recounts the Tarahumara and Toltec legends about the origin of corn. Included is a description of how to make cornhusk puppets. Vivian Blackmore's *Why Corn Is Golden* retells a legend about the color of corn. *Why There Is No Arguing in Heaven* by Deborah Nourse Lattimore relates the Mayan legend of the Maize God who created the first men and women from maize kernels. Older students can read Tony Hillerman's *The Boy Who Made Dragonfly*, which retells a Zuni creation myth and talks of a boy who made the first dragonfly out of cornhusks.

The school librarian or media specialist can help locate many books and other materials about international foods. Activities centered around cooking and food can be extended throughout the year. Regional recipes can be kept in country files; menus can be collected from books, parents, and ethnic restaurants. With the support of adults at home, students can be encouraged to bring in ethnic foods to share with the class.

Clothing is another theme for engrossing research to promote diversity education. The picture book *Hats, Hats, Hats* by Ann Morris blends the purposes and occasions for wearing hats in different countries. Humorous photos depict hats for play, work, warmth, and protection from the elements. J.H. Hahn's *Seven Korean Sisters* describes the origin of the sakdong chogri, which Korean women wear on special occasions. *Cornrows* by Camille Yarbrough poetically describes the richness of the African custom that calls for a story to be told while hair is being braided into cornrow patterns.

Seasonal celebrations are common to all cultures. Lila Perl and Alma Ada's *Piñatas and Paper Flower/Piñatas y Flores de Papel*, written in both English and Spanish, describes several holidays celebrated in various parts of the Americas. Included are discussions of the New Year, Three Kings' Day, Carnival, Easter, and Halloween. Bernardino de Sahagun's *Spirit Child* is a fascinating Nativity tale written in the 1500s, after Spain had conquered Mexico. Barbara Cooney's beautiful illustrations depict the Nativity with Aztecs as the main characters. *Rosita's Christmas Wish* by Mary-Ann Bruni tells the story of a nine-year-old girl who wants to play a part in a traditional Mexican Christmas drama. Especially interesting for children who may have recently moved to the United States is *Diane Goode's American Christmas*. This book can be used to introduce American poems, songs, and well-known stories with a Christmas theme.

Fiction and nonfiction about holiday traditions unique to other cultures can expand children's awareness of the world. *Hanukkah!* by Roni Schotter shows the joy and festivities of this Jewish holiday as experienced by five young children, while *The Story of Hanukkah* by Amy Ehrlich retells the Biblical story and is boldly illustrated with symbols of the Jewish faith. *Lion Dancer: Ernie Wan's Chinese New Year* by Kate Waters and Madeline Slovenz-Low depicts a six-year-old Chinese boy who dances his first Lion Dance on the streets of New York City. Brilliant photographs capture the excitement of Ernie, his proud family, and the Chinese community through the preparations for and celebration of this festival. Books like these will do much to show children both the wonderful diversity of the world and the many similarities that exist among peoples from different cultures.

The Oral Tradition

All cultures have an oral tradition through which stories, wisdom, and history are passed from generation to generation. Folk literature provides children with a window on the storytelling traditions of different cultures as well as on their own. Many children enrolled in North American schools today come from cultures where reading is practiced only by a privileged few. Storytelling is the means by which many learn about customs, values, and family and cultural history. Teachers can model reading and convey the importance and value of books. Choosing to tell stories from the oral tradition of different cultures will ease the transition from oracy to literacy. All students, but especially second language learners, can benefit from this approach.

In whatever form, traditional stories tell us much about the cultures in which they originate. In *Ashanti to Zulu* (Musgrove), for example, we learn that in Africa there is a Baule legend that tells of a queen's sacrifice to save her people. Tomie dePaola's *The Legend of the Bluebonnet* tells of an Indian child who sacrifices her doll in order to end drought and famine to save her people. To connect these stories to children's own experiences teachers can ask what a

20th-century adult or child would sacrifice for the good of the community. What are the values in our classroom? Our school? Our families?

Folktales told in two languages are particularly useful in classrooms where children have different first languages. Joe Hayes provides both English and Spanish in his books. His *Mariposa, Mariposa* or *La Llorona* can be read in both languages or told in either language to give students broader exposure. *Cuentos: Tales from the Hispanic Southwest* by José Griego y Maestas and translated by Rudolfo Anaya is an appropriate English/Spanish book for older students.

Refrains make stories easy to tell and perfect for audience participation. Janina Domanska's *Busy Monday Morning,* a Polish folk song with the repeated phrase "And so did I," can be easily translated into students' primary languages. With the help of parents and native speakers, students and teachers can master the pronunciation of the refrain in a number of languages. Wanda Gag's *Millions of Cats,* an American classic, is a good example of a patterned language story that can be easily translated. *Cientos de gatos, miles de gatos, millones y billones y trillones de gatos* simply sounds exciting. Giving a Korean child the opportunity to model for teacher and classmates a Korean translation of a refrain, for example, will build self-esteem enormously. Using a child's primary language for refrains enhances self-awareness, self-esteem, and validates the importance of the individual's culture.

The Human Condition

If children meet book characters who are from other cultures but who have emotions or experiences similar to their own, they begin to understand that, in spite of differences, people share a common humanity. When diversity education teachers celebrate the ethnicity of each student, they also create an atmosphere of community and acceptance in the classroom. Students at all grade levels are encouraged to express their feelings about human experiences and emotions by writing in journals or through discussions.

Most young children are in an ethnocentric stage of cultural awareness when they begin school, generally because they have had little exposure to people outside their family's own circle of friends and relatives. Picture books such as *Angel Child, Dragon Child* by Michele Surat help them develop a broader awareness. This particular book will also help children become more aware of their own cultural heritage. Ut, a Vietnamese child, is a new and "different" student. Other children make fun of the "pajamas" she wears and laugh when she speaks English. Ut's loneliness and feelings of alienation offer readers an opportunity to evaluate their feelings and attitudes toward those who are different from themselves.

A number of books develop the theme of nonacceptance. In Min Paek's *Aekyung's Dream,* Aekyung, a Korean girl, is teased about being "Chinese." She is finally accepted when her classmates learn she has a talent for painting. *Victor* by Clare K. Galbraith depicts the distress of a young boy whose mother doesn't come to school events because she can't speak English. In Barbara Cohen's *Molly's Pilgrim,* Molly suffers anguish when her mother dresses her pilgrim doll in a Russian costume instead of traditional American colonial garb. It is particularly touching when Molly's mother tells the child that she, too, is a pilgrim who came to America in search of religious freedom.

In these books, rejection becomes acceptance. In real life, of course, it takes more than one event or the reading of one story for most children to embrace one another. Through numerous literary encounters, discussions, and opportunities to write, children begin to realize that we are all capable of hurting others through ignorance and also of avoiding such hurt by coming to value diversity.

Books on specific topics include Barbara Hazen's *Tight Times,* a picture book about poverty and joblessness. Hunger, both physical and emotional, is the theme of *The Jazz Man* by M.H. Weik, a book suitable for primary and intermediate children. Camille Yarbrough's *The Shimmershine Queens* is about two fifth-grade girls whose powerful dreams and aspirations transcend the harshness of their urban environment. *Daydreamers* by Eloise Greenfield is a wonderfully illustrated mood piece that emphasizes the importance of dreaming for developing self-awareness. Beautiful folk art illustrates Anne Pellowski's *The Nine Crying Dolls,* a favorite Polish tale about a baby who won't stop crying. For primary students, this book can serve as an introduction to *I Am Not a Crybaby!* Author Norma Simon's exceptional multicultural picture book examines why children and adults cry.

Books that deal with the suffering brought on by war enhance children's understanding of the ultimate consequences of hatred and ignorance. *Fire from the Sky,* edited by William

Vornberger, is a moving account of children living with civil war in El Salvador. Pictures drawn by orphaned children depict a story of unbearable horror. Despite this, the book closes on a note of hope—the faith in the future that these victims, living in destitute surroundings in Honduran refugee camps, share.

The promise of a brighter future is the theme of *I Never Saw Another Butterfly,* edited by Hana Volavkova. The material in this book was written and illustrated by children who perished at the Terezin concentration camp during World War II. The back cover states: "These are the voices which have been preserved, the voices of reminder, of truth, of hope." *Memories of My Life in a Polish Village, 1930-1949* is Toby Fluek's memoir of village life told from her perspective as a young Jewish girl who lives through peace, war, and finally liberation and immigration to the United States. Brilliant paintings and poignant text convey the joy and sorrow of Fluek's life. Shizuye Takashima's *A Child in Prison Camp* is an autobiographical account of a Japanese Canadian girl's internment in a relocation camp during World War II.

Any of these books could stimulate research and writing projects in which students interview children or adults who have experienced war.

The Universal Declaration of Human Rights: An Adaptation for Children (by Ruth Rocha and Otavio Roth) serves as a culminating activity for explorations into our shared human condition. A quote from this book could be the watchword for all diversity education teachers: "Education should emphasize understanding, comprehension, tolerance, and friendship."

Transcending the Limits

Every child, teacher, librarian, parent, and author has a unique view of the world; the classroom is the place their views converge. The level of commitment to multiculturalism achieved by each member of the classroom community plays an important role in fostering a global perspective for everyone. Diversity education provides teachers and students with the opportunity to transcend the limits imposed by ethnocentricity. As Cole (1991) states so well, "We are for difference. For respecting difference. For allowing difference until difference doesn't make any more difference."

References

Cole, J. (1991, March). *Achieving the promise in diversity.* Address presented at "Difficult dialogues: Achieving the promise of diversity," National Conference on Higher Education, Washington, DC.

Diakiw, J.Y. (1990). Children's literature and global education: Understanding the developing world. *The Reading Teacher, 43,* 296-300.

Evans, C. (1987). Teaching a global perspective in the elementary schools. *Elementary School Journal, 87,* 545-555.

García, R.L. (1982). *Teaching in a pluralistic society: Concepts, models, strategies.* New York: HarperCollins.

Children's Books

Aliki. (1976). *Corn is maize: The gift of the Indians.* New York: Crowell.

Bang, M. (1983). *Ten, nine, eight.* New York: Greenwillow.

Bang, M. (1985). *The paper crane.* New York: Greenwillow.

Berdan, F.F. (1989). *The Aztecs.* New York: Chelsea House.

Bernardo, S. (1981). *The ethnic almanac.* Garden City, NY: Doubleday.

Berrill, M. (1989). *Mummies, masks, and mourners* (Time detective series). New York: Lodestar.

Blackmore, V. (1981). *Why corn is golden: Stories about plants.* Boston, MA: Little, Brown.

Bruni, M.S. (1985). *Rosita's Christmas wish.* San Antonio, TX: TexArt Services.

Bunting, E. (1982). *The happy funeral.* New York: Harper Junior.

Coerr, E.B. (1977). *Sadako and the thousand paper cranes.* New York: Dell.

Cohen, B. (1983). *Molly's pilgrim.* New York: Lothrop, Lee & Shepard.

dePaola, T. (1983). *The legend of the bluebonnet: An old tale of Texas.* New York: Putnam.

Domanska, J. (1985). *Busy Monday morning.* New York: Greenwillow.

Durell, A. (1989). *The Diane Goode book of American folk tales and songs.* New York: Dutton.

Egypt in pictures. (1988). (Visual geography series; ill. by S. Feinstein). Minneapolis, MN: Lerner.

Ehrlich, A. (1989). *The story of Hanukkah.* New York: Dial.

Elwood, A., & Madigan, C.O. (1989). *The Macmillan book of fascinating facts: An almanac for kids.* New York: Macmillan.

Fagan, B.M. (1984). *The Aztecs.* New York: Freeman.

Fluek, T.K. (1990). *Memories of my life in a Polish village, 1930-1949.* New York: Knopf.

Gag, W. (1928). *Millions of cats.* New York: Coward-McCann.

Galbraith, C.K. (1971). *Victor.* Boston, MA: Little, Brown

Goble, P. (1989). *Beyond the ridge.* New York: Bradbury.

Goode, D. (1990). *Diane Goode's American Christmas.* New York: Dutton.

Greenfield, E. (1981). *Daydreamers.* New York: Dial.

Griego, M.C. (1981). *Tortillitas para mamá and other nursery rhymes, Spanish and English.* New York: Holt, Rinehart & Winston.

Griego y Maestas, J. (1980). *Cuentos: Tales from the Hispanic Southwest* (trans. by R.A. Anaya). Santa Fe, NM: Museum of New Mexico Press.

Hahn, J.H. (1980). *Seven Korean sisters.* Los Angeles, CA: Institute for Intercultural Studies.

Hayes, J. (1986). *La llorona.* El Paso, TX: Cinco Puntos.

Hayes, J. (1988). *Mariposa, Mariposa.* Santa Fe, NM: Trails West.

Hazen, B.S. (1983). *Tight times.* New York: Puffin.

Hillerman, T. (1986). *The boy who made dragonfly: A Zuni myth.* Albuquerque, NM: University of New Mexico Press.

Isberg, E. (1989). *Peak performance: Sports, science, and the body in action.* New York: Simon & Schuster.

Kinney, J., & Kinney, C. (1976). *23 varieties of ethnic art and how to make each one.* New York: Atheneum.

Lattimore, D.N. (1987). *The flame of peace: A tale of the Aztecs.* New York: HarperCollins.

Lattimore, D.N. (1989). *Why there is no arguing in heaven: A Mayan myth.* New York: HarperCollins.

Meltzer, M. (1977). *Never to forget: The Jews of the Holocaust.* New York: Dell.

Meltzer, M. (1981). *The Chinese Americans.* New York: Crowell.

Meltzer, M. (1982). *The Hispanic Americans.* New York: Crowell.

Meltzer, M. (1982). *The Jewish Americans: A history in their own words.* New York: Crowell.

Meltzer, M. (1984). *The Black Americans: A history in their own words.* New York: Crowell.

Meltzer, M. (1988). *Rescue: The story of how Gentiles saved Jews in the Holocaust.* New York: Harper Junior.

Meltzer, M. (Ed.). (1990). *The American promise: Voices of a changing nation, 1945-present.* New York: Bantam.

Miles, M. (1971). *Annie and the old one.* Boston, MA: Little, Brown.

Morey, J., & Dunn, W. (1989). *Famous Mexican Americans.* New York: Dutton.

Morris, A. (1989). *Bread, bread, bread.* New York: Lothrop, Lee & Shepard.

Morris, A. (1989). *Hats, hats, hats.* New York: Lothrop, Lee & Shepard.

Moss, J., & Wilson, G. (Eds.). (1989). *Peoples of the world: Latin Americans.* Detroit, MI: Gale.

Musgrove, M. (1976). *Ashanti to Zulu: African traditions.* (Ill. by L. Dillon & D. Dillon.) New York: Dial.

Odijk, P. (1989). *The Egyptians* (Ancient world series). Englewood Cliffs, NJ: Silver Burdett.

Oliphant, M. (1989). *The Egyptian world.* New York: Warwick.

Paek, M. (1988). *Aekyung's dream.* San Francisco, CA: Children's Book Press.

Pellowski, A. (1980). *The nine crying dolls.* New York: Philomel.

Perl, L., & Ada, A.F. (1983). *Piñatas and paper flowers/Piñatas y flores de papel: Holidays of the Americas in English and Spanish.* New York: Clarion.

Ploski, H.A., & Williams, J. (Eds.). (1989). *The Negro almanac: A reference work on the Afro American.* Detroit, MI: Gale.

Politi, L. (1976). *Three stalks of corn.* New York: Scribner's.

Porter, A.D. (1991). *Jump at the sun: The story of Zora Neale Hurston.* Minneapolis, MN: Carolrhoda.

Rocha, R., & Roth, O. (1989). *The universal declaration of human rights: An adaptation for children.* New York: United Nations.

Sahagun, B.D. (1984). *Spirit child.* (Trans. by J. Bierhorst; ill. by B. Cooney.) New York: Morrow.

Schotter, R. (1990). *Hanukkah!* Boston, MA: Little, Brown.

Simon, N. (1989). *I am not a crybaby!* Niles, IL: Albert Whitman.

Surat, M.M. (1983). *Angel child, dragon child.* New York: Scholastic.

Takashima, S. (1971). *A child in prison camp.* Montreal, P.Q.: Tundra.

Time-Life Books Staff. (1990). *Feats and wisdom of the ancients* (Library of curious and unusual facts series). Alexandria, VA: Author.

Turner, D. (1989). *Bread.* Minneapolis, MN: Carolrhoda.

Unterburger, A.L., & Delgado, J.L. (Eds.). (1990). *Who's who among Hispanic Americans.* Detroit, MI: Gale.

Volavkova, H. (Ed.). (1987). *I never saw another butterfly: Children's drawings and poems from Terezin concentration camp* (trans. by J. Nemcova). New York: Schocken.

Vornberger, W. (Ed.). (1986). *Fire from the sky: Salvadoran children's drawings.* New York: Writers and Readers Publishing Cooperative.

Waters, K., & Slovenz-Low, M. (1990). *Lion dancer: Ernie Wan's Chinese New Year.* New York: Scholastic.

Weik, M.H. (1966). *The jazz man.* New York: Atheneum.

West, J.O. (1988). *Mexican-American folklore.* Little Rock, AR: August House.

White, F.M. (1973). *César Chávez: Man of courage.* Champaign, IL: Garrard.

Yarbrough, C. (1979). *Cornrows.* New York: Coward-McCann.

Yarbrough, C. (1989). *The shimmershine queens.* New York: Putnam.

Chapter 3

Factual History:
Nonfiction in the
Social Studies Program

Betty Carter
Richard F. Abrahamson

Teachers of social studies and teachers of language arts and reading are natural allies. In elementary school, one person is often both social studies teacher and literacy teacher; social studies and language arts teachers were among the first to team up to offer the interdisciplinary classes that are now so much a part of the middle school movement. Today these two groups of teachers have much in common: just as the reading and language arts curriculum in many schools is moving toward a literature-based approach, elementary and middle school social studies curricula are moving in the same direction. Social studies teachers, like their literacy counterparts, have found that literature infuses their lessons with new life and motivates students to study and learn. The lagniappe, or unexpected bonus, of such programs occurs when students also find pleasure in these books, pleasure that for many may be the first step in becoming a lifetime reader.

Although much has been written about the use of trade books (books other than textbooks or reference materials) in the social studies program, the idea is anything but new. Referring to a 1988 study, McGowan and Guzzatti write, "Since 1929, over 160 sources have explicated the ways in which trade books can enrich social studies teaching" (1991, p. 16). Many of these articles focus on using historical fiction, folktales, and biographies, but literature is more than these three genres and does more than tell narrative stories. Literature in its many forms can organize facts, present powerful opinions, introduce new theories, provide directions, and allow readers to sequence information, compare and contrast data, search for causes and effects, and structure knowledge in a variety of ways.

For centuries, a whole range of literary forms has drawn our attention to what was, what is, and what can be. The diverse writings of such people as John Locke, Martin Luther, Abraham Lincoln, Jane Addams, Anne Frank, Karl Marx, Bob Woodward, Carl Bernstein, and Barbara Tuchman have not only recorded the human experience, but have also defined it. From Thomas Paine's *Common Sense* to Simone de Beauvoir's *The Second Sex* to Martin Luther King, Jr.'s *Letter from a Birmingham Jail,* nonfiction—with its stirring language, compelling subjects, and impressive ability to provoke thought and challenge beliefs—has shaped philosophies, societies, and individuals. To ignore expository prose, essays, diaries, letters, and factual accounts in the classroom is to deny the very roots of the human heritage social studies hopes to teach. Yet when nonfiction is mentioned in the professional literature, the emphasis is on biography, folklore, and fables—nonfiction's narrative component. Other nonfiction offerings, what we will refer to as "informational books" in this chapter, are typically discussed with much less enthusiasm and are recommended less frequently as books for pleasure reading.

The California Department of Education's *Literature for History: Social Science, Kindergarten through Grade Eight* (1991) typifies the kind of bias we mean. In the introduction to this annotated list of books for social studies the authors state, "One of the most popular kinds of literature represented herein is historical fiction" and "Biography is an especially powerful genre for young readers, not only for the light it sheds on the past but also for examples of human understanding." Fables are described as "superb material for helping children think about the consequences of behavior" (pp. ix-x). Words such as "popular," "powerful," and "superb" certainly are strong, appropriate adjectives to use to describe these genres, but compare them to what the authors write about informational books:

> A range of nonfiction [informational books] is included for the purposes of general interest, student research, and alignment with specific content in framework units. These titles can help form a nucleus of nontextbook library materials that support the framework's curriculum. A number of these books can serve as teachers' background material as well (p. xi).

The lack of enthusiasm for informational books is obvious. "Superb," "popular," and "powerful" are replaced with "student research," "general interest," "nontextbook library material," and "background material."

We believe that along with fables, historical fiction, and biography, informational books for children and young adults can be superb, popular, and powerful. Some social studies scholars have also begun to discuss the importance of informational books in the social studies curriculum and to warn against a program based too extensively on narrative. Levstik, for example, persuasively argues that "history is more than narrative. It is also learning to sift evidence before it has been shaped and interpreted" (1992, p. 13). She goes on to write:

> Questions of fact and interpretation raised in this context can be used to initiate historical inquiry, refer students to other sources (including a solid array of informational texts), and provide a forum for the presentation of student interpretations. This, I think, is a crucial and often overlooked component to thinking and learning history. Certainly the students I have studied were enthusiastic participants in such inquiries. Even in the first grade, students valued their role as "researchers" and made regular use of a variety of informational texts. This

type of mediation also helps guard against the uncritical acceptance of literary constructions of history. The power of narrative is not an unmitigated good (pp. 13-14).

Beyond covering social studies subject matter, informational books provide hours of enjoyment for many children. Preschool youngsters freely choose informational books to read (Childress, 1985), and as they grow older, they select even more nonfiction (Blair, 1974; Carter & Abrahamson, 1990; Fader & McNeil, 1968; Norvell, 1973; Purves & Beach, 1972). By the high school years, at least half of young adults' reading is nonfiction (Ellis, 1987). All too frequently, though, it is assumed that these books are checked out of libraries to supplement a class assignment or to help with a research report. Often that assumption is not true: the circulation patterns in school libraries indicate that informational books children take home frequently have little relationship to the curriculum (Abrahamson & Carter, 1992; Beers, 1990).

A literature-based social studies program that ignores nonfiction ignores the major reading interests and preferences of many children and young adults. Further, from a teaching standpoint, it leaves out some of the best written and most effective literature available for young readers. Historical fiction and folktales are an accepted part of the literature-based social studies movement, but nonfiction informational books have the power to play an equally important role if we let them. That is what this chapter is all about.

The Reader's Approach

With literature-based social studies programs, teachers hope their students will learn about the excitement of discovery, the nature of society, and the accomplishments and failures of humankind through vivid accounts that make history, economics, sociology, and geography come alive. Teachers also hope to introduce reading material that encourages children to make active responses to books and develop the habit of reading. In the past, children learned the content from textbooks and any excitement, personal identification, or active response came from outside reading in trade books. But when outstanding trade books are the core of the social studies curriculum, these distinctions become blurred. Readers don't simply absorb facts from informational books and they don't read fiction exclusively to trigger emotional responses.

Good literature, no matter what its form, encourages and sometimes demands a variety of responses from its readers. A fine book offers some youngsters the means to explore a discipline, others a resource for discovering information, and still others a chance to identify with people or situations.

Readers interact with texts in one of two ways: they either look for what they can carry away from the text or they look for what they can experience through the text. The assumption that informational books, with their facts and details, provide the former while narrative, with its characters and storylines, provides the latter implies that the text determines readers' stance. In practice, the reverse is true. Some children, for example, make powerful individual responses to the social studies content in historical fiction. These are the youngsters who read a book such as Christopher and James Lincoln Collier's *My Brother Sam Is Dead* and contemplate, as does the young protagonist, the futility of war. They may ask, "How could the horrors of the American Revolution have happened?" and question the necessity of any armed conflict. Some may extend these questions to ask, "What can I do to prevent society from allowing such atrocities to happen again?" Other readers, however, may have the same sort of reaction to Barbara Rogasky's informational book *Smoke and Ashes: The Story of the Holocaust*. They may study her expository prose and find power in its recounting of the facts about the millions of people who were persecuted, tortured, and murdered. These readers may even ask the same questions: "How could these horrors have happened? What can I do to prevent society from allowing such atrocities to recur?" Neither author nor literary form dictate these responses; the readers do.

Fiction and informational books can also offer readers the means to find themselves in literature. Harold Keith's *Rifles for Watie*, one of the most outstanding fictional accounts available about the American Civil War, prompts many readers to identify with Jefferson Davis Bussey, a young farm boy from Kansas who joins the Union army. They see the experiences of war through his eyes and contrast his reactions with what they think their own might be. Other readers, however, see young Bussey only as a "made-up" character who reacts merely as the author wishes him to. These readers may make a more personal identification with people depicted in informational books. They may read Jim Murphy's *The Boys' War*, a discussion of the various ways in which young children participated in the Civil War, and identify with their historical counterparts. Some may see themselves in Elisha Stockwell, for example, a Wisconsin youth whose father and sister objected loudly to his volunteering for the Union army. For many young adults, Stockwell's frustration and anger strike a chord with their own struggles to make independent and mature decisions, leading them to wonder what they would do if they found themselves in Stockwell's position. Would they be impetuous and defiant or would they submit to their parents wishes? If they enlisted, would they be brave or cowardly soldiers?

Yet another group of children may identify not with historical figures but with the society in which these men and women lived. They may read of the conditions in hospitals where injured Civil War soldiers were treated, for example, and wonder if they could summon the courage to cope with the primitive medical methods, as a patient, a surgeon, or a nurse. Such questions give readers a personal stake in the events of a historical period—not as memorizers of facts and dates, but as active participants in their own heritage.

Rich nonfiction provides many opportunities for identifying with characters and situations. The frontispiece of Nicholas Reeves's *Into the Mummy's Tomb*, for example, shows the wooden head of the boy king Tutankhamun emerging from a lotus. His vulnerable face and regal carriage may appeal to some readers, the enlarged holes in his ears may interest others, while the statue's obvious decay may prompt yet others to consider the carelessness with which outsiders invaded this young Pharaoh's tomb. Readers' associations may well shift when they discover that the author first developed an avid interest in Egyptology as a teenager. And as the book details Howard Carter's opening the tomb and seeing "wonderful things," readers may well imagine themselves in that situation. Would they, like Carter, have made a surreptitious trip to the tomb the night before the opening? Would they have the patience to catalog each artifact in the first chamber before moving deeper insider to uncover other treasures? Would they be tempted to sneak some of the objects out of Egypt and keep them hidden at their homes as Lord Carnarvon did? With each shift of identity, readers experience a new perspective and a different point of view, thus enlarging their grasp on history and society.

Still other readers may prefer to participate more actively in books. These are the youngsters who tune out Russell Freedman's well-crafted descriptions of Lincoln's tortured soul in *Lincoln: A Photobiography,* but may enjoy re-creating his anguish in a portrait they sketch with the assistance of Lee J. Ames' *Draw Fifty Famous Faces.* Their personal stances will come not by identifying with a real or fictional person, but rather by creating meaning while physically responding to a popular informational book.

We must remember that children who master a particular subject and become lifelong readers in the process, are those who somehow find something personal within the pages of books. In order to trigger these responses, teachers and librarians must provide a variety of books through which their students can explore a discipline, discover information, and identify with the issues and individuals who define the content area.

Reading Aloud

Providing a variety of books for children to read is the starting point for encouraging them to interact with all kinds of literature. The second step is to help young readers learn to value literature. One of the best ways to do this with respect to informational books is to incorporate them into the classroom read-aloud program. Since fiction is the traditional choice for classroom read-alouds, introducing nonfiction may require a brief transition period. Teachers and children alike may want their first experiences with nonfiction to contain the comfortable elements of narrative stories. Fortunately, the wealth of fine informational books now being published offers many appropriate choices.

In *Mush! Across Alaska in the World's Longest Sled-Dog Race,* Patricia Seibert emphasizes that narrative structure with the opening line "This is the true story of an unusual race" (1992, p. 5). The true story begins with the first inhabitants of Alaska, the Inuit, and with the sled dogs they trained; it continues to chronicle the discovery of gold and the settlement of Nome, just south of the Arctic Circle. Listeners will hear about the plight of those isolated pioneers, who had their lives threatened by an outbreak of diphtheria in 1925. No medicine was available locally, "so a relay of sled-dog teams was sent racing across the frozen wilderness, carrying the precious medicine. Nome was saved" (p. 11). In 1973, to honor this historic feat, Joe Redington inaugurated the first Iditarod, an annual race in which mushers and their dog teams follow the thousand-mile route from Anchorage to Nome. A particularly appropriate read-aloud for primary children, *Mush!* offers young listeners accurate history, a fascinating discussion of the Iditarod, and, best of all, a good story.

Jean Fritz, a master of narrative in nonfiction, underscores the drama inherent in history in her account of the 6,000-mile journey of Mao Zedong's army in *China's Long March*. Her introduction resembles the beginning of a powerful play:

> The story opens in 1934. By this time Chiang Kai-Shek's Nationalist regime was recognized by most foreign countries as the legal government of China. But not by the Communists. In the interior of China they were building up their army and spreading their revolution among the peasants. They were still determined to take over China.
>
> The scene is Jiangxi, a remote mountainous province in southern China. The danger is about to begin (p. 12).

Older students lucky enough to hear *China's Long March* will follow the soldiers across China's raging rivers, over perilous mountains, and through vast, empty grasslands. They will meet men and women who undertook an incredible ordeal because they saw it as necessary for instigating much-needed change in their country. And they will come to know and perhaps share the passions of individuals such as Xiauxia, a young woman who fought courageously for opportunities for women, or Little Xie, a victim of the battle of Loushan Pass who delighted in writing and producing original plays. Since many of the names in *China's Long March* may be unfamiliar to students, teachers may want to display a pronunciation guide while reading this particular book aloud; displaying a map helps students with the geography of the Long March.

Once children and teachers are comfortable with informational books as read-alouds, the selections can be broadened. As Levstik reminds us, "The power of narrative is not an unmitigated good" (1992, p. 14). Just as the books available in the classroom should reflect a variety of structures and genres, so should those chosen for read-alouds. Diane Hoyt-Goldsmith deftly combines story narrative with exposition in *Arctic Hunter*. This book introduces listeners to Reggie, a ten-year-old Inupiat who lives in

Kotzebue, Alaska. He describes his family's annual summer trek to a camp on Sadie Creek where they hunt and fish for food to sustain them through the following winter. Each chapter discusses an aspect of that trip, from the break-up of the ice around Kotzebue to the methods of fishing and preserving food to the games the children play. Some children will use Reggie's journey to organize the information they hear while others will depend on the topical outline to guide their listening, but *Arctic Hunter* will provide both groups with a satisfying experience.

Similarly, Russell Freedman's *Children of the Wild West* blends narrative elements with expository prose. This account of how children lived, worked, went to school, and played on the American frontier does not follow the experiences of a single child, but presents a picture of what life must have been like for many pioneer youngsters. The book is organized by topics such as "Going West," "Frontier Schools," and "Building the West." Freedman's use of diaries, journals, and archival photographs brings a range of individuals into the center of this compelling read-aloud.

Listeners should never be passive, but some read-aloud selections demand more energetic participation than others. In *Guess Again: More Weird & Wacky Inventions*, Jim Murphy introduces a series of less than memorable inventions that have clogged the patent office, such as an overcoat for two people, a mechanical dance partner, and an air-cooled reclining rocking chair. But Murphy doesn't *tell* us what these gizmos are, he asks us to guess. For each contraption he provides a description, an illustration, and a choice of possible uses. To guarantee an interactive read-aloud, the teacher or a student can read the background material, show the accompanying diagram, and ask listeners to figure out the purpose of each device. *Guess Again* is both instructive and entertaining but should be taken only in small doses; after a while the guessing game becomes repetitive. This is the kind of book to keep in the classroom to share with students whenever a couple of spare minutes crop up during the day.

In fact, one of the beauties of many informational books is that they excerpt well. Teachers may choose to read a chapter or section every now and then over a long period of time or instead read a single segment as a way of introducing a book. Reading aloud only brief segments is a good way to emphasize or extend some part of the social studies curriculum. For example, a highly compelling account of slavery comes in Walter Dean Myers's *Now Is Your Time! The African-American Struggle for Freedom*. In the second chapter, Myers outlines the fate of Abd al-Rahman Ibrahima, an African prince who was ambushed, brought to America, and sold as a slave:

> A few months before, he had been a learned man and a leader among his people. Now he was a captive in a strange land where he neither spoke the language nor understood the customs. Was he never to see his family again? Were his sons forever lost to him?
>
> As a Fula, Ibrahima wore his hair long. Foster [his owner] insisted that it be cut. Ibrahima's clothing had been taken from him, and his sandals. Now the last remaining symbol of his people, his long hair, had been taken as well.
>
> He was told to work in the fields. He refused, and he was tied and whipped. The sting of the whip across his naked flesh was terribly painful, but it was nothing like the pain he felt within. The whippings forced him to work.
>
> For Ibrahima this was not life, but a mockery of life (© 1991 by Walter Dean Myers, p. 20; reprinted by permission).

Just as reading aloud should not be restricted to fiction and biography, neither should it be confined to third-person accounts. Russell Freedman (1992) describes a government employee who had traveled with the Freedom Train Museum that visited many cities across the United States. One night, after the exhibit had closed, he succumbed to an irresistible temptation: he sat in Lincoln's rocker. Later, he privately confessed that he felt like an eyewitness to history. By using first-person accounts in the classroom, teachers can give students the same feeling. No matter how dramatic, secondary sources filter the social studies. Students will benefit by coming in contact with original material, but since primary sources frequently contain arcane language and unfamiliar sentence constructions, teachers can best introduce them by reading aloud.

In *The American Revolutionaries*, Milton Meltzer makes diaries, letters, and other personal records accessible to modern students. He introduces each document, firmly setting each in its historical context. The result is a history alive with the people and ideas from the revolutionary period. For example, the dreadful conditions of crossing the Atlantic in those days are detailed in Gottfried Mittelberger's 18th-century writings:

> Pitiful signs of distress—smells, fumes, horrors, vomiting, various kinds of sea sickness, fever, dysentery, headaches, heat, constipation, boils, scurvy, cancer, mouth-rot, and similar afflictions, all of them caused by the age and the highly salted state of the food, especially of the meat, as well as by the very bad and filthy water, which brings about the miserable destruction and death of many. Add to all that shortage of food, hunger, thirst, frost, heat, dampness, fear, misery, vexation, and lamentation, as well as other troubles. Thus, for example, there are so many lice, especially on the sick people, that they have to be scraped off the bodies (p. 6).

Such original material naturally excerpts well, and fortunately also reads aloud well.

Not all the original material read aloud to children needs to be as somber as the above example, however. Humor is a natural component of the human experience and should therefore find a home in the social studies classroom. The following excerpt from James Cross Giblin's *From Hand to Mouth*, gives children a droll view of the 15th century. Quoting from *On Civility*, Erasmus's book of manners, Giblin lists several rules for proper conduct while eating:

> Take care to cut and clean your fingernails before dining. Otherwise dirt from under the nails may get in the food.
> Don't be the first to reach into the pot; only wolves and gluttons do that. And don't put your whole hand into it—use only three fingers at most.
> Take the first piece of meat or fish that you touch, and don't poke around in the pot for a bigger one.
> Don't pick your nose while eating and then reach for more food.
> Don't throw bones you have chewed back in the pot. Put them on the table or toss them on the floor.
> Don't clean your teeth with your knife.
> If your fingers become greasy, it is not polite to lick them or wipe them on your coat. Bring a cloth along for this pur-

pose if your host does not provide one. Or else wipe them on the tablecloth (© 1987 by James Cross Giblin, pp. 30-32; reprinted by permission).

Informational books like these deserve to be read aloud, and teachers can incorporate these books into their social studies programs both easily and naturally. The payoff comes when students learn to value all sorts of books or welcome the introduction of an unfamiliar genre that may well expand their own reading choices. As one fourth grader in Houston, Texas, wrote about his feelings after hearing informational books: "Well, I thought it was going to be boring. That it was going to be bad. Well, now I said to myself I was wrong. I think that it is grate reading nonfiction. I didn't read nonfiction. I read nonfiction now" (Gabriel, 1992, p. 10).

Blurring the Lines

In reviewing James Cross Giblin's *Let There Be Light* in the *Bulletin of the Center for Children's Books,* Roger Sutton wrote, "Social commentary runs fluently throughout: why Moslems constructed windows that allowed one to see out but not in; the differences between cultures that build windows facing a courtyard and those that build them facing the outside. This is as much a history of how people live as it is a history of windows" (1988, p. 71). Fine nonfiction books present pieces of information as they appear in the real world—not as discrete facts but as inter-related data that together can influence nations, communities, and individuals. Outstanding informational books naturally cross curriculum boundaries; that is, they discuss not just facts about something like the scientific breakthroughs in window-making technology, but the history of the many peoples who have looked through windows. David Macaulay's books on various constructions (*Pyramid* and *Mill*, for instance) are particularly good examples of texts that blur the lines between subject matter in the social studies, science, and art.

By using literature with such a broad focus, teachers may counter the oft-repeated charge that children are not helped to transfer skills and information from one subject area to another. Frequently educators and parents complain that youngsters don't transfer their understanding of the writing process to their history assignments or don't use skills learned in math when working out percentages in science class or don't transfer reading skills that deal with maps, charts, and graphs when they see these figures in their geography textbooks. But why *should* students be able to transfer skills in these ways? Schools with rigid departments and inflexible scheduling contradict the very concept. For many children, only informational books blend the disciplines they have so energetically studied as separate entities.

Sometimes this blending occurs in the process of research, as it does in Brent Ashabranner's *Dark Harvest*. Here the author uses the methods of participatory observation from anthropology in order to try to make sense of the complex social and political structure of today's migrant society. He lives with and interviews a variety of people, asks them how the economics of their lives have shaped their political and social outlooks, and wonders about solutions to the problem of the underemployed. Ashabranner helps develop what Jean Fritz refers to as the "watcher" in children: "One of the purposes in presenting the past is to develop the *watcher* in children, for the living of life and the watching of life are bound by one cord" (1981, p, 86). Nowhere is that role of the watcher more dramatically emphasized than in books such as *Dark Harvest*, whose authors share their process of observation.

Frequently the overlapping of different disciplines comes through a book's scope. In *The Smithsonian Book of Flight for Young People*, Walter Boyne traces technological progress in aviation but he doesn't simply list events in a vacuum. Instead, he draws powerful parallels between the nature of war and the nature of airplanes as weapons. He shows how in the early days of flight, the aviation industry around the world formed partnerships with the military, business, and government. He describes how technological advances ultimately changed the nature of war, the geopolitical landscape of Europe, and the functioning of nations after World War II. In this one book, science, economics, history, politics, and sociology all blend much as they do in our complex modern world.

Since the social studies reflects the actions of humankind, the literature used to teach about it should underscore the interdependence of people, events, and societies. *Eight Hands Round*, an alphabet book that uses the names of quilt patterns for each of the letters, deftly weaves the history of the United States into the art of its ancestors. In each entry, author Ann Paul introduces a patchwork pattern, details its design, and gives a speculative explanation about its origin from American history. In *Buffalo Hunt,* Russell Freedman takes an important ritual and shows how its various components have been interpreted in art. But Freedman doesn't just ask readers to observe, he asks them to think: about the symbols of a nation and the ways in which those symbols were destroyed; about the sophisticated rituals used in the hunt and the unsophisticated destruction of that way of life; and about the complex way art depicts life. Bringing art into the social studies with books like these not only links the disciplines but also affords students fresh perspectives about history.

Informational books for the social studies also reach into the language arts. Etymologies and eponyms spark units on holidays in Peter R. Limburg's *Weird! The Complete Book of Halloween Words* and Lynda Graham-Barber's *Gobble! The Complete Book of Thanksgiving Words*; *Mushy! The Complete Book of Valentine Words*; and *Doodle Dandy! The Complete Book of Independence Day Words.* With these entertaining volumes readers can discover the origins of symbols (such as Uncle Sam and Cupid), the history of words (such as "turtledove" and "ghost"), and the origins of the sorts of celebrations now held on holidays such as Thanksgiving and the Fourth of July.

Building Literary Ladders

Of course, the most frequently mentioned use of informational books is to provide background material. Although we don't advocate this as the exclusive purpose of such books, we don't want to neglect its importance. Consider, for example, Pam Conrad's *Prairie Songs,* a historical novel often taught in elementary language arts classrooms. It tells the story of Louisa, a young girl living in a sod house on the barren and desolate Nebraska prairie. While her life is satisfying, it isn't exciting—at least, not until the new doctor and his beautiful wife, Emmeline, come to stay. It is from Emmeline that Louisa learns about the beauty of books, language, and poetry. Less directly, it is also from Emmeline that Louisa learns about her own strength to endure and triumph. Setting is crucial to this book, and Conrad sets the scene beautifully in the first paragraph.

The prairie was like a giant plate, stretching all the way to the sky at the edges. And we were like two tiny peas left over from dinner, Lester and me. We couldn't even see the soddy from out there—just nothing, nothing in a big circle all around us. We still had Cap then, and he stood very still, shaking his harness now and again while we did our work, throwing chips into the back of the wagon, me singing all the time (pp. 1-2).

But Conrad's poetic introduction means little to those youngsters who possess limited knowledge of U.S. history and are consequently ill-equipped to visualize her carefully wrought scene. In order to provide children with concrete images before they start reading, teachers can turn to nonfiction books—in this case, perhaps to Russell Freedman's *Children of the Wild West*, which can provide background crucial to understanding *Prairie Songs*.

Figure 1, taken from *Children of the Wild West*, shows two youngsters engaged in the activity Pam Conrad describes in the

Figure 1
Gathering Cow Chips in the Late 1890s

Reproduced by permission of the Nebraska State Historical Society.

opening of *Prairie Songs*—gathering cow chips. The barren prairie stretches in an almost endless line, the children's broad brimmed hats indicate that the sun is baking down on them; and their obvious burden shows students that the life of pioneer children was not an easy one. Here is the kind of background youngsters need to appreciate Conrad's metaphor comparing the vast prairie to an empty dinner plate.

Informational books not only provide background for this fine novel, they can also extend it. During the first third of *Prairie Songs*, a photographer named Soloman Butcher visits Louisa's family. As he explains to the family, he is "putting together a book—a book about courage and endurance":

> He turned gently and extended his arm to all of us. "A book about you...."
> They [Butcher's photographs] are recorded history. As it happens. Preserved for all time, the faces and lives of the people of this country. "Look." He pointed to a horse that stood beside a soddy in one of the photographs. "Look at the ribs on that animal. Hard times. Yes, indeed. Hard times. And they won't be forgotten now, not the faces, or the animals, or the rolling hills" (pp. 57-68).

At the close of *Prairie Songs*, Louisa's family attends a local Fourth of July celebration. There they discover Mr. Butcher's photographs on display—pictures of family after family who settled and survived in Nebraska. In 1991, six years after the publication of *Prairie Songs*, Pam Conrad published *Prairie Visions: The Life and Times of Solomon Butcher*. This informational book outlines the life of this real-life photographer in a handsome volume liberally sprinkled with pictures of early settlers, like fictional Louisa and her family. In this literary ladder, a nonfiction book provides background for a fictional account, which in turn provides the background for another nonfiction volume.

Along with providing background material for some books and springboards into others, informational books also give children ideas about writing. The organizational patterns of alphabet books like Jim Aylesworth's *The Folks in the Valley*, which presents customs and activities of the Pennsylvania Dutch, or Jonathan Hunt's *Illuminations*, which introduces readers to the Middle Ages, remind young authors that their own writing can take forms other than narrative. In addition, various techniques used by authors of informational books are worth noting. For example, in *The Great St. Lawrence Seaway*, Gail Gibbons discusses the history of the Great Lakes region, its transportation system, and the construction and operation of various locks. But many interesting tidbits of information—such as the fact that the St. Lawrence Seaway is closed about three months a year because of the weather or that it took 15,000 people to build the seaway—don't fit into this text. By including such facts in a separate appendix, Gibbons indirectly shows students how to focus their writing but still add other material that may interest an audience.

Learning from Illustrations

In *Prairie Songs*, Louisa and her family don't really know how to look at the photographs Solomon Butcher shows them. They are unable to see beyond the immediate images to what the photographs say about their own lives, their environment, and their courage. Like Louisa, elementary children frequently fail to look beyond the immediate scene when they see illustrations. After all, much of their contact with photographs has probably involved looking through a family album. They see themselves as babies, Aunt Tillie at her daughter's wedding, and the entire family gaily waving at their summer campsite. Photographs can tell more than who and where the subjects are, but only if children know how to look at them.

Many outstanding informational books depend on well-chosen photographs, art prints, and original drawings to clarify and extend their text. Teachers can easily help youngsters develop strategies for comprehending visual material. Figure 2 provides an example. In it are two photographs we found in Russell Freedman's *Children of the Wild West* along with statements based on Raphael's (1984) "Question Answer Relationships," or QARs. Raphael states that "what really matters is knowing what information sources are available for seeking a correct answer" (p. 303). Her experiences with elementary children show that by focusing on the demands of the question—whether the answer comes directly from the text, whether it can be inferred from the text, or whether it can only come from looking outside the text—teachers can help

Figure 2
Finding Information in Illustrations

Back row, left to right: Tis-chaf-un (Laughing Face)—Arickaree; Say-ed-da (White Brest)—Mandan; U-hah-ke-um-pa (Carries Flying)—Blackfoot Sioux; E-corrupt-ta-ha (Man who looks around)—Mandan; Ka-ru-nack (Sioux Boy)—Arickaree. *Second row, left to right:* Koo-nook-te-wan (Sharphorn)—tribe not listed; Mok-pi-a Ma-ni (Walking Cloud)—Unkpapa Sioux; Pa Ma-ni (One who hoots when he walks)—Unkpapa Sioux; A-hu-ka (White Wolf)—Arickaree. *Front, seated:* Ari-hotch-kish (Long Arm)—Gros Ventre.

Back row, left to right: Say-ed-da; U-hah-ke-um-pa; E-corrupt-ta-ha; Ka-ru-nack. *Second row, left to right:* Tis-chaf-un; Pa Ma-ni; A-hu-ka. *Front, seated:* Ari-hotch-kish.   *(continued next page)*

Carter & Abrahamson

Figure 2 (continued)

Look at the two photographs on the previous page. The first one is a group of Indian boys on their arrival at Hampton, Virginia, in November 1878. The second shows many of the same boys approximately 15 months later.

- -

Right there. Check the statements that can be confirmed by the two pictures or their captions.

____ 1. Ten Indian boys came to school in Hampton, Virginia, in 1878.

____ 2. The Arickaree are an Indian people.

____ 3. The Indian boys had their hair cut while they were in school.

____ 4. Each Indian Nation used a distinctive blanket to identify itself.

Think and search. Check the statements that make sense to you after looking at the pictures.

____ 1. The Indian boys in these pictures left their homelands to attend school.

____ 2. The school in Hampton respected the national traditions of these Indian boys.

____ 3. These boys were proud to be chosen to attend school.

____ 4. The Sioux were the dropouts of the 19th century.

On your own. Put a check by the statements that you feel apply to this school in 1878 and to schools today. If you think the statements apply only to 1878, put a Y in the blank. If you think the statements apply only to today, put a T in the blank.

____ 1. The high school years are the happiest of a teeanger's life.

____ 2. Schools respect the worth of the individual.

____ 3. Going to school is preparation for life.

____ 4. To be a success, one must fit into the mainstream of society.

Photographs reproduced by permission of the National Anthropological Archives, Smithsonian Institution.

youngsters look at the task requirements of questions, begin to understand the differences between information sources, and improve the quality of their answers. What we've suggested here is that such sensitivity to responses be extended to searching for information in illustrations.

In *Prairie Visions*, Pam Conrad tells readers that on one occasion Solomon Butcher drew a turkey atop a soddy in order to cover up a damaged negative.

> The story goes that when Butcher delivered the photograph, the homesteader stared at the photo and said, "What is that?"
>
> Butcher answered, "Why, it looks like a turkey to me."
>
> "Couldn't be a turkey," the homesteader said. The turkeys weren't around that day. Besides...we don't have any white ones."
>
> The homesteader's wife drew near and looked at the photo too. "Yes, Theodore," she said. "don't you remember me telling you to drive the turkeys away? (pp. 19-20).

Children should learn not to easily accept the turkeys they see in photographs and on their television screens; teachers must encourage them to examine graphics both critically and carefully. A.J. Wood's *Errata: A Book of Historical Errors* provides an excellent introduction to this idea. In 12 color plates, illustrator Hemesh Alles adds ten mistakes—such as interspersing the alphabet with Egyptian hieroglyphics, displaying a Christmas tree at a Norman feast, and showing a faucet spewing out water at an Inuit camp. He invites readers to look carefully at each picture and find as many mistakes as they can. If they are stumped or if they wonder about some of the elements in the pictures (Would the Chinese have used wheelbarrows in building the Great Wall? Do oak trees grow in Egypt? Did the Moguls play cricket in the 16th century?) they can turn to the back where each object is shown *in situ* and explanations are provided. This book is a good step up the reading ladder for scores of Waldo fans.

Youngsters can learn to use their visual literacy skills when they select books as well as when they read them. Book jackets are a kind of advertising, a literary "hard sell" akin to what children see on billboards and televisions. Publishers and authors want readers to notice their books at bookstores and therefore often make considerable efforts to produce appealing covers. But do the jackets give a fair preview of the contents?

The jacket illustration for Milton Meltzer's *Rescue: The Story of How Gentiles Saved Jews in the Holocaust* (shown in Figure 3) showcases a dramatic scene: A man fiercely battles heavy seas, his small craft bulges with terrified passengers, and the menace of the Nazi swastika hovers in the background. This is certainly an attention-grabbing cover, and in this case the illustration accurately reflects the tone of the book. A different mood is created by the two soldiers on the jacket of *Voices of the Civil War*, also by Milton Meltzer. These young men appear ordinary—as if the camera had caught them in the middle of a march or while resting at a bivouac. Readers will note that one soldier comes from the Union Army while the other is a Confederate. Both their allegiances and their informality give clues to the content of the book—a collection of diary entries, letters, and public records of the people who participated in the Civil War. They provide a fitting glimpse into a volume about the everyday hopes and dreams of individuals recorded amid the drama of war.

Figure 3

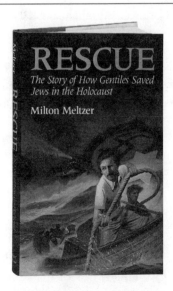 

Covers of *Rescue*, ©1988 by Milton Meltzer, and *Voices of the Civil War*, ©1989 by Milton Meltzer. Reproduced by permission of HarperCollins Publishers.

One final point about illustrations. Many of the photographs used in informational books come from museums and libraries. These institutions often will reproduce their photographs in enlarged sizes or as slides for use in the classroom, and they will do so at a nominal fee. Teachers need only notice the picture credits or acknowledgments in informational books and contact the original sources to see if they offer such services. Students can follow the same process to find appropriate visuals to complement their research or to incorporate in their social studies assignments.

Asking Questions, Building Understanding

Teachers often confess that they want to introduce informational books in their classrooms, but they feel uncomfortable asking questions about them. As one reading specialist confided, "When I'm talking to students about fiction, I have some standard questions I can fall back on to start their thinking. I can ask about plot, setting, characters, or a number of other features. But when it comes to nonfiction, I don't know what to ask beyond 'What was the book about?' or 'Did you enjoy it?'" Many teachers just aren't used to examining informational books and shy away from asking children to take a critical look at the genre.

The following questions, adapted from a longer series we developed for junior high students (Carter & Abrahamson, 1990), are offered as starting points for initiating discussion about informational books.

Which illustrations do you wish you had created yourself? Why? How would you have made them? Here children are asked to examine the illustrations—not in terms of content, but rather in terms of execution. What would students have to do in order to re-create the perspective David Macaulay employs when drawing the great pyramid? Would they have to visit Egypt, climb the pyramid, or just have an active imagination? When readers take photographs of wilderness areas on family camping vacations, do they resemble Richard Hewlet's work for Caroline Arnold's *The Ancient Cliff Dwellers of Mesa Verde*? How are they alike? How are they different?

Compare this nonfiction book with another one on the same topic. How do they differ? How are they alike? Which one do you like better or believe more? Why? This series of questions allows students to examine different sources; to look for conflicting information or points of view, to think about organizational patterns, scope, and depth of presentation; and to compare the veracity of each work. For example, youngsters get one picture of the Battle of Gettysburg from Alden Carter's expository account in *The Battle of Gettysburg*, another in the comparison of the war journals of Confederate soldier John Dooley and Union soldier Thomas Galway in Jim Murphy's *The Long Road to Gettysburg*, and yet another in Neil Johnson's *The Battle of Gettysburg*, a discussion of the battle as seen through the 125th anniversary reenactment. These questions also create a natural opportunity for teachers and librarians to explore individual reading habits so they can recommend related books.

What kind of teacher do you think the author would make? In *Beyond Fact: Nonfiction for Children and Young People*, Carr (1982) compares fine nonfiction authors to gifted teachers. The analogy is apt. Children understand and respond to informational books that are clear, interesting, and well written. This question will help young readers decide whether the discussion of Champollion's scholarship makes sense to them in James Cross Giblin's *The Riddle of the Rosetta Stone*; whether they understand how a system of locks operates after reading Gail Gibbons's *The Great St. Lawrence Seaway*; or whether they know the definitions of "continental divide," "mesa," or "atoll" after reading Jack Knowlton's *Geography from A to Z*. By answering and asking this kind of question, children begin to define the partnership that exists between readers and authors.

What did you learn from this book that wasn't found in your social studies textbook? Here youngsters look at the difference between sources. They can see how a book such as Leonard Everett Fisher's *The White House* personalizes the lives of the presidents; how Caroline Arnold's *A Guide Dog Puppy Grows Up* talks about the community by introducing a young girl who volunteers to care for a puppy and then relinquishes the dog to the professionals who train seeing-eye dogs; and how in Isadore Seltzer's *The House I Live In* children are shown living in houseboats, Victorian mansions, adobes, and mobile homes, all sharing a concept of home. These observations underscore the important notion that no one book holds all the answers, or even all the questions, in the social studies.

What is the most important word in this book? Why? The intention of this particular question is not to resurrect painful "main idea" exercises, but rather to have children share their lasting impressions of a book. The responses to this question will always vary as much as do the readers and the books they choose. Some children will read Beatrice Siegel's *The Year They Walked: Rosa Parks and the Montgomery Bus Boycott* and think of the word "courage"; others may come up with "sacrifice," "energy," or "organization," while still others will mention "oppression," "violence," or "bigotry." These kinds of concepts will start a small group talking about the book, the ideas contained in it, and their own reactions to a period in history.

A Powerful Tool

In searching for the best trade books for literature-based social studies programs, let's not neglect informational books for children. For many youngsters these books offer both enrichment in the content of social studies as well as enjoyable reading. By reading aloud informational books, by showing youngsters how they can learn from the illustrations in the books, by asking good questions about these books, and by making sure we praise children as much for the nonfiction reading they do as for their fiction reading, we'll move informational literature beyond the category of simple "background material" and discover that it can have the same power as fiction. In the process, the social studies program will become richer and our students will have more opportunities to read, discuss, explore, and learn.

References

Abrahamson, R.F., & Carter, B. (1992). What we need to know about nonfiction and young adult readers and what we need to do about it. *Publishing Research Quarterly, 8,* 41-54.

Beers, G.K. (1990). *Choosing not to read: An ethnographic study of seventh-grade aliterate students.* Unpublished doctoral dissertation, University of Houston, Houston, TX.

Blair, J. (1974). *The status of nonfiction in the reading interests of second, third, and fourth graders.* Unpublished master's thesis, Rutgers University, New Brunswick, NJ. (ED 095 481)

California Department of Education. (1991). *Literature for history: social science, kindergarten through grade eight.* Sacramento, CA: Author.

Carr, J. (1982). *Beyond fact: Nonfiction for children and young people.* Chicago, IL: American Library Association.

Carter, B., & Abrahamson, R.F. (1990). *Nonfiction for young adults: From delight to wisdom.* Phoenix, AZ: Oryx.

Childress, G. (1985). Gender gap in the library: Different choices for boys and girls. *Top of the News, 42,* 69-73.

Ellis, W.G. (1987). To tell the truth or at least a little nonfiction. *ALAN Review, 14,* 39-40.

Fader, D.N., & McNeil, E.B. (1968). *Hooked on books: Program and proof.* New York: Berkley.

Freedman, R. (1992). Fact or fiction? In E.B. Freeman & D.G. Person (Eds.), *Using nonfiction trade books in the elementary classroom* (pp. 2-10). Urbana, IL: National Council of Teachers of English.

Fritz, J. (1981). *The very truth.* In B. Hearne & M. Kaye (Eds.), *Celebrating children's books* (pp. 81-86). New York: Lothrop, Lee & Shepard.

Gabriel, M. (1992). *Sharing the read-aloud throne with fiction: Children respond to listening to nonfiction read aloud regularly.* Unpublished manuscript, University of Houston, Houston, TX.

Levstik, L.S. (1992). *Mediating content through literary texts: Mediating literary texts in elementary classrooms.* Paper presented at the Annual Meeting of the American Educational Research Association, San Francisco, CA.

McGowan, T., & Guzzatti, B. (1991). Promoting social studies understanding through literature-based instruction. *Social Studies, 82,* 16-21.

Norvell, G. (1973). *The reading interests of young people.* East Lansing, MI: Michigan State University Press.

Purves, A.C., & Beach, R. (1972). *Literature and the reader: Research in response to literature.* Urbana, IL: National Council of Teachers of English.

Raphael, T.E. (1984). Teaching learners about sources of information for answering comprehension questions. *Journal of Reading, 27,* 303-311.

Sutton, R. (1988). [*Review of* Let there be light: A book about windows]. *Bulletin of the Center for Children's Books, 42,* 71.

Children's Books

Ames, L.J. (1974). *Draw fifty famous faces.* Garden City, NJ: Doubleday.

Arnold, C. (1991). *A guide dog puppy grows up.* San Diego, CA: Harcourt Brace Jovanovich.

Arnold, C. (1992). *The ancient cliff dwellers of Mesa Verde.* New York: Clarion.

Ashabranner, B. (1985). *Dark harvest: Migrant farm workers in America.* New York: Putnam.

Aylesworth, J. (1992). *The folks in the valley: A Pennsylvania Dutch ABC.* New York: HarperCollins.

Boyne, W.J. (1988). *The Smithsonian book of flight for young people.* New York: Atheneum.

Carter, A.R. (1990). *The battle of Gettysburg.* New York: Watts.

Collier, J.L., & Collier, C. (1974). *My brother Sam is dead.* New York: Four Winds.

Conrad, P. (1985). *Prairie songs.* New York: HarperCollins.

Conrad, P. (1991). *Prairie visions: The life and times of Solomon Butcher.* New York: HarperCollins.

Fisher, L.E. (1989). *The White House.* New York: Holiday House.

Freedman, R. (1983). *Children of the wild west.* New York: Clarion.

Freedman, R. (1987). *Lincoln: A photobiography.* New York: Clarion.

Freedman, R. (1988). *Buffalo hunt.* New York: Holiday House.

Fritz, J. (1988). *China's long march: 6000 miles of danger.* New York: Putnam.

Gibbons, G. (1992). *The great St. Lawrence seaway.* New York: Morrow.

Giblin, J.C. (1987). *From hand to mouth: Or, how we invented knives, forks, spoons, and chopsticks, & the table manners to go with them.* New York: Crowell.

Giblin, J.C. (1988). *Let there be light: A book about windows.* New York: Crowell.

Giblin, J.C. (1990). *The riddle of the Rosetta Stone: Key to ancient Egypt.* New York: Crowell.

Graham-Barber, L. (1991). *Gobble! The complete book of Thanksgiving words.* New York: Bradbury.

Graham-Barber, L. (1991). *Mushy! The complete book of Valentine words.* New York: Bradbury.

Graham-Barber, L. (1992). *Doodle dandy! The complete book of Independence Day words.* New York: Bradbury.

Hoyt-Goldsmith, D. (1992). *Arctic hunter.* New York: Holiday House.

Hunt, J. (1989). *Illuminations.* New York: Bradbury.

Johnson, N. (1989). *The battle of Gettysburg.* New York: Four Winds.

Keith, H. (1957). *Rifles for Watie.* New York: Crowell.

Knowlton, J. (1988). *Geography from A to Z: A picture glossary.* New York: Crowell.

Limburg, P. (1989). *Weird! The complete book of Halloween words.* New York: Bradbury.

Macaulay, D. (1975). *Pyramid.* Boston, MA: Houghton Mifflin.

Macaulay, D. (1983). *Mill.* Boston, MA: Houghton Mifflin.

Meltzer, M. (1987). *The American revolutionaries: A history in their own words.* New York: Crowell.

Meltzer, M. (1988). *Rescue: How Gentiles saved Jews in the Holocaust.* New York: HarperCollins.

Meltzer, M. (1989). *Voices from the Civil War.* New York: Crowell.

Murphy, J. (1986). *Guess again: More weird & wacky inventions.* New York: Bradbury.

Murphy, J. (1990). *The boys' war: Confederate and Union soldiers talk about the Civil War.* New York: Clarion.

Murphy, J. (1992). *The long road to Gettysburg.* New York: Clarion.

Myers, W.D. (1991). *Now is your time! The African-American struggle for freedom.* New York: HarperCollins.

Paul, A.W. (1991). *Eight hands round: A patchwork alphabet.* New York: HarperCollins.

Reeves, N. (1992). *Into the mummy's tomb: The real-life discovery of Tutankhamun's treasures.* New York: Scholastic.

Rogasky, B. (1988). *Smoke and ashes: The story of the Holocaust.* New York: Holiday House.

Seibert, P. (1992). *Mush! Across Alaska in the world's longest sled-dog race.* Brookfield, CT: Millbrook.

Seltzer, I. (1992). *The house I live in: At home in America.* New York: Macmillan.

Siegel, B. (1992). *The year they walked: Rosa Parks and the Montgomery bus boycott.* New York: Four Winds.

Wood, A.J. (1992). *Errata: A book of historical errors.* New York: Green Tiger Press.

Carter & Abrahamson

Chapter 4

Literature Adds Up for Math Class

Diana Cohn
Sara J. Wendt

Over the past three years of teaching together at the Little Red Schoolhouse in Manhattan, we have worked to create an exciting integrated curriculum for our fourth grade students. This was fairly readily accomplished in the language arts program: our students see themselves as real readers and authors because they are actively involved in meaningful reading and writing activities. Our classroom is a community and, with guidance and suggestions from us, the children in our community read and write in ways that interest them. They choose reading material from a collection of trade books and write for real audiences. Linking these sorts of activities to social studies and science was easy enough. Our students regularly read texts related to these content areas and write about their explorations.

It was quickly obvious to us that our language arts, social studies, and science programs succeeded in grabbing our students' interests, but we felt our math program needed to be restructured in order to be just as challenging and engaging for them. When it came to math, our students just didn't see themselves as real problem solvers. In this respect our math program was isolated from the rest of the curriculum.

We decided to experiment with restructuring our math program so that, as in our integrated reading and writing programs, our students would learn mathematical concepts in a real and meaningful context. In order to do this, we brought reading and writing into our math lessons. We began by asking our students to keep logs in which they wrote about their strategies for solving math problems. They shared their strategies, reading aloud excerpts from their logs just as they would read aloud an excerpt of creative writing during our "writing share" time. We also asked the students to create and write down their own math problems by drawing on real-life experiences or events described in children's literature and to read and solve the problems written by their classmates. After a few weeks of modest success, we decided to use children's literature more directly in our math program. This proved to be an excellent move: modeling mathematical concepts by means of examples from favorite books immediately attracted our students' attention and enlivened math class.

Our modest success and desire to gain more ground prompted us to do a presentation for our colleagues. This was easy to organize because the faculty meets once a week to discuss issues related to the school, the classrooms, and individual students. This time is often used for sharing success stories or discussing problems. Staff members work as a team to develop curricula that are integrated not only within each classroom but across the grades.

We began our presentation with an example of how we use William Steig's *The Real Thief* to add interest to a lesson on subtraction and reinforce concepts of regrouping. We read the following passage to the staff:

> Naturally, whenever the King removed anything from the treasury, or added anything to it, he informed Gawain of the changes.... For a long time, nothing was amiss.... But one day, in his routine checkup, it seemed to Gawain that the pile of rubies was smaller than it should have been. He counted

hastily and went flapping and running to the King to report
that something was missing.... He put down his pot of honey,
wiped his fingers, and together they went back to the treasury.

By the light of a lamp they carefully counted the rubies,
both calling out the numbers. Sure enough, there were only
8,643 of the red gems when there should have been 8,672.

Our colleagues couldn't resist calculating—just as our fourth
graders had been unable to resist doing—that there were 29 jewels
missing from the king's treasury.

As we shared other examples, we found that some of our
colleagues were already using children's literature in their math
programs and were eager to describe their successes; in fact, the
use of trade books is a thread that runs throughout the lower school
math curriculum. We thought it would be useful to document children's experiences with math and literature at our school, so we
asked our colleagues to provide two or three examples of how they
use trade books in their math programs. What they told us helped
us refine our own program and provided what we thought might be
useful suggestions for other teachers.

Math + Literature = Success

Twenty-two six-year-old children read loudly in unison:
"'No one makes cookies like Grandma,' said Ma as the doorbell
rang." Then first grade teacher Bonnie Glass turned the page of a
Big Book version of *The Doorbell Rang* by Pat Hutchins. The story
begins with mother handing her two children, Sam and Victoria, a
plate of 12 chocolate chip cookies she has just baked. They are
pleased to determine that when they divide the delicious cookies,
they will each get six. But then the doorbell rings and two more
children come in. Sam and Victoria now have to share their 12
cookies with Tom and Hannah, and each child will receive three
instead of six. The doorbell keeps ringing and each time as more
friends arrive Sam and Victoria lose out on more cookies. Finally
Grandma arrives with a new batch of cookies.

As Bonnie read the story aloud with her students, her assistant, Jim Occhino, worked with the students at the flannelboard.
Children eagerly came to the flannelboard to act out each phase of

the story, solving the mathematical problems as they arose by dividing the felt cookies among the characters.

Bonnie and Jim extended this activity with a cooking lesson. First Bonnie wrote a recipe for chocolate chip cookies in large print on chart paper and asked the students to help her read it aloud. And then the math part began. Noel measured 1 cup of chocolate chips while Kosiya measured 1 cup of sugar. Maya measured 1 teaspoon of vanilla and Jackie measured ½ cup of butter. Bonnie and Jim helped the children measure all the ingredients and gave them a concrete demonstration of how quantities relate to one another—*twice* as much flour as sugar, for example. The children took turns blending the ingredients at various stages in the recipe. Then two children were asked to spoon the cookie dough onto the cookie sheets, placing it in four rows of six cookies each. After the cookies were baked, the children were asked to work together to divide them so that each student received the same number, just as Sam and Victoria had had to do in Pat Hutchins's story.

Sorting and classifying is another math-related skill practiced repeatedly in many first grade classrooms. Bonnie and Jim's students sorted everything: sea shells, marbles, cubes, and buttons. "The Lost Button," a story from Arnold Lobel's *Frog and Toad Are Friends*, is perfect for introducing a lesson in sorting and classifying. In the story, Toad loses a button and Frog wants to help him find it, but each time Frog finds a button and enthusiastically brings it to Toad, it seems that it has the opposite characteristic from the one Toad lost. Toad responds throughout the story in the following pattern:

> That button is black, my button was white.
> That button has two holes, my button had four holes.
> That button is small, my button was big.
> That button is square, my button was round.
> That button is thin, my button was thick.

Toad finally finds his white, four-holed, big, round, thick button on the floor at home.

After reading the story, the first graders began sorting and classifying activities to make distinctions among a large variety of buttons. Two children played a game in which one partner sorted buttons into trays. In one tray Frances put only black and blue buttons with two holes and in the other she put the remaining buttons. Then Frances's partner, Nina, had to discover the classification pattern Frances had chosen.

A book Bonnie found useful for introducing a lesson on counting was *Two Ways to Count to Ten: A Liberian Folktale,* retold by Ruby Dee. In this story, the king of the jungle is a leopard who can count from one to ten in the time it takes him to throw a spear into the air and catch it again. When he grows old, he says to all the other animals, "Some day when I am gone, another king must rule in my place. I will choose him now from among you so that he will be ready." He decides on a contest: the animal who can send a spear so high that he can count to ten before it comes down again will become the new king. Many animals try and fail until the shrewd antelope comes along. When he throws the stick high in the air, he dances and then shouts, "Two, four, six, eight, ten!"

The children loved this clever solution to the problem. Bonnie then spent the remainder of the math class asking her students to count to ten by grouping different manipulatives to form different sequences. The students, motivated by their delight in a trade book, were eager to experiment and discover the patterns possible in numbers.

Jenny Kramer, a second grade teacher, incorporates folktales, fairy tales and nursery rhymes into her math curriculum each year. The children read these stories throughout the year on their own, and Jenny also reads them aloud. The children use the characters and plots of these familiar stories to write their own math problems.

Here are some examples of how Jenny's second graders incorporated fairy tales into a unit on fractions:

- Jack and Jill went up the hill to fetch a pail of water. Then they filled it half way up, but a quarter leaked out. How much is left?

- What fraction of the three little pigs live in the brick house?

- Humpty Dumpty broke into 1,000 pieces. All the king's men put together 500 pieces of him. What fraction of the pieces were put together?

- In *The Three Bears*, what fraction of the three bears have hot porridge?
- If there were 25 women at the ball in *Cinderella*, what fraction of the women at the ball did the prince like?

The children are enthusiastic about solving one another's problems because they are extracted from stories that have meaning for them and are creatively written by their peers.

Jenny also uses folktales and fairy tales to teach students about graphing. One year Jeremy questioned his peers about their reactions to a number of fairy tales and then made a bar graph to show the group's favorite characters; Sophie took a survey and made a picture graph showing the children's most despised fairy tale personality. This activity helps children understand how graphs give a visual display of information and asks them to use their analytic skills by determining and explaining why they like or despise different characters.

Every spring Jenny does a unit on money. She finds that this study is always successful because, she believes, it provides information that is relevant to the children's lives. Jenny begins the unit by working with her students to identify and give specific values to coins and bills. The children then do numerous activities in which they count coins and figure out different ways of combining them to make a specified total. Children might, for example, determine the different ways they could make a dollar from four quarters, five dimes, six nickels, and five pennies.

One year in the middle of the unit, the children proposed opening their own restaurant. Jenny encouraged their creativity and thought of specific ways to relate running the restaurant to math and the money unit. Some students rehearsed being waiters, calculating the total cost of their classmates' meals and practicing making change; others pretended to be cost-conscious customers, working out how much they could spend; other children practiced being competent cashiers. When everyone was ready, the restaurant "opened," serving food the children had brought from home. Adding up bills and making change became real.

Jenny waits until the end of the money unit to read *Alexander, Who Used to Be Rich Last Sunday* by Judith Viorst. The children enjoy the humor of this book and are eager to point out all the mistakes Alexander makes with his $1.00 bill. The children, with their new-found understanding of money and its value, feel like experts and know that they, unlike Alexander, would make wise choices about spending.

Third grade teacher Grace Cohen uses her students' shared experience of stories when she introduces the concept of time. She begins the unit by asking her class, "Who remembers the story *The Very Hungry Caterpillar?*" The children's eyes light up as they remember this favorite story from when they were "little." The book describes the diet of a hungry caterpillar over the course of a week, before its two-week incubation in a cocoon and subsequent emergence as a beautiful butterfly. Grace uses the children's recollections of the story to open a discussion about intervals of time. "How long is a year?" she asks. "A month? A week?" Her students answer her questions by telling her how many days fit into each time period. Then she asks, "How long is a day?" The children now move into discussing hours, minutes, and seconds.

To add humor to the unit on time, Grace usually reads Pat Hutchins's *Clocks, Clocks, and More Clocks*, a tale about a man who discovers that he needs to have a watch in order to set the clocks on the different floors of his four-story house. Grace also reads *Solomon Grundy, Born on Oneday: A Finite Arithmetic Puzzle* by Malcolm E. Weiss. This book is filled with teaching ideas for exploring mathematical concepts in the calendar.

Grace extends her unit on time by integrating it with a social studies unit on explorers and a science unit on the solar system. The explorers use the stars as reference points for navigating and telling time. By studying the rotation of the earth in relation to the sun, Grace's students deepen their understanding of time intervals.

Learning from Our Colleagues

Our investigations about our colleagues' use of literature in their math classes gave us many ideas for refining and invigorating our own program. First, although these teachers were working with children in first through third grade, we felt that at least some of the books they used could be incorporated into our fourth grade curriculum. After all, it is our experience that elementary students at all levels share a love of good stories and well-illustrated picture books. For example, we now use *Alexander, Who Used to Be Rich*

Last Sunday, popular in Jenny Kramer's second grade, as a reminder to our fourth graders to be wise spenders. We extend this into a discussion of money and, as a class, we read together David M. Schwartz's *If You Made a Million*. The book shows the varied forms money can take and is especially useful for showing how money can be used to make purchases. This book can be applied to more advanced work in units having to do with interest and percentages.

To give children a sense of responsibility for their "own" money, we allot them all a make-believe bank balance and ask them to balance their checkbooks by subtracting each time the amount of the "purchases" they make. The children are quickly motivated to practice subtraction by imagining they can buy all the things they might wish for. They use their estimating skills to figure out the price of what they wish to buy and to see if they can afford the item given their individual bank balances. When they discover they can afford the item, they fill in the checkbook entry as an adult would and subtract the amount from the previous total.

Our success with linking literature to math led us to explore possible connections across our overall curriculum. We found it easy to integrate math concepts naturally into our social studies curriculum, which itself has many links to our language arts program. For example, each year our students study the history of the Taino people of the Caribbean and the consequences of Christopher Columbus's arrival. In addition to doing a macro-timeline spanning 2000 years and documenting the arrival of the Tainos in the Caribbean from South America, the students also create a micro-timeline depicting the personal and pivotal events in Columbus's life. Their reference for this activity is *Where Do You Think You're Going, Christopher Columbus?* by Jean Fritz. As they extract information about Columbus's life and voyages, many questions arise. These, in turn, lead to discussions and extension projects about time, distance, maps, and navigation. One year, the fourth graders asked to write their own autobiographies describing the major events in their nine years.

By the end of fourth grade, we expect our students to have strong skills in and understanding of multiplication. (Indeed, throughout the grades at our school, students are encouraged to look for the patterns in numerical relationships.) *Anno's Mysterious Multiplying Jar* by Mitsumasa Anno beautifully engages students in perceiving the remarkable numerical relationships in multiplication and probability. Once this book inspired three of our stronger math students to try to figure out how many different seating arrangements were possible for four students and four desks.

Toward the end of the school year, our fourth graders study fractions. We generally begin all our math units by encouraging students to experiment with manipulatives. During the fraction unit, we especially like to use a variety of math games that incorporate pattern blocks to review and reinforce fractional relationships. We encourage our students to observe and record all the different ways they see fractional relationships in their lives. For example, Nora observed that telling time has fractional components, Clarence observed how fractions are used in advertisements for sales, Regina saw fractional relationships in money, and Larry saw fractions in recipes and cooking. Next we ask the students to write story problems for one another using their everyday experience with fractions. Anthony came up with this one:

> McKays Drug Store is having a sale on Nintendo games. If the price of a Nintendo game is $50.00 and the sale tag says ¼ off, then how much is the price of the Nintendo game?

During the fraction unit we read aloud *The 17 Gerbils of Class 4A* by William H. Hooks. In this story, three friends decide to share a litter of gerbils in the following way: Tommy is to own ½ of them; Cynthia is to own ⅓ of them; and Chris is to own ⅑ of them. The problem in the story is that there are 17 gerbils and it is impossible to divide them in these proportions. At the end of the book the students learn the humorous solution to the problem—if they haven't figured it out before then!

While our students are studying fractions in math, they are also studying the ecology of the rainforest in social studies. "Rainforest math" now connects these two units. The students participate in a simulation game in which they have to determine what the future will be for a given piece of the rainforest. They have to look at the total acreage of the property and then determine what part will be reserved for different interest groups. They choose what percentage of the total rainforest property will be sold to a pharmaceutical company, a lumber company, a cattle company, and a tourist conservation company, and which part the native population will retain. This group problem-solving activity involves much discussion and negotiation in order to make difficult decisions.

In addition to using trade books to teach explicit math skills, we use children's literature to teach math concepts. Just as Jenny's second graders use folktales, fairy tales, and nursery rhymes to write interesting math problems for their peers, our fourth graders read trade books and engage in the same kind of process. During our study of animal adventure stories the students read *The Trumpet of the Swan* by E.B. White. As an extension activity we use this book to motivate our students to write their own addition, subtraction, multiplication, and division problems. For example, Joseph created this problem:

> It takes 35 days for trumpeter swans to hatch and a swan usually lays six eggs. If there are 17 swans in a northern Canadian lake, how many cygnets will be born in 35 days?

Shawanda wrote:

> If Louis played 36 notes per minute on his trumpet, how many notes would he play during a 3-hour concert on a swan boat in the Public Garden in Boston?

We find that math problems based on children's literature are more popular than the traditional textbook-type word problems. We believe that by using characters and events from stories children know provides a meaningful, shared reference point and increases motivation to solve problems.

Finally, we keep a copy of *Anno's Math Games II* by Mitsumasa Anno available in our classroom. It includes sections on all aspects of mathematical problem solving with obvious teaching opportunities. Inspired by some of the picture puzzles in the book, our students create their own math puzzles with which to challenge one another. This book will motivate math explorations for elementary students at all levels.

Finding Fun in Math

Throughout this chapter we have cited different ways teachers have incorporated children's literature in their math programs. We hope that these examples demonstrate the many possibilities for and benefits of integrating math with trade books and perhaps may inspire different teaching ideas.

Do our students now see themselves as problem solvers? We asked them this question during a math lesson at the end of the year. The measure of our success was in their resounding cheer of "Yes! Math is really fun!"

Children's Books

Anno, M. (1983). *Anno's mysterious multiplying jar.* New York: Philomel.

Anno, M. (1989). *Anno's math games II.* New York: Philomel.

Carle, E. (1983). *The very hungry caterpillar.* New York: Philomel.

Dee, R. (Reteller). (1990). *Two ways to count to ten: A Liberian folktale.* New York: Holt.

Fritz, J. (1981). *Where do you think you're going, Christopher Columbus?* New York: Putnam.

Hooks, W.H. (1976). *The 17 gerbils of class 4A.* New York: Coward-McCann.

Hutchins, P. (1970). *Clocks, clocks, and more clocks.* New York: Macmillan.

Hutchins, P. (1986). *The doorbell rang.* New York: Greenwillow.

Lobel, A. (1970). *Frog and Toad are friends.* New York: HarperCollins.

Schwartz, D.M. (1989). *If you made a million.* New York: Lothrop, Lee & Shepard.

Steig, W. (1976). *The real thief.* New York: Farrar, Straus & Giroux.

Viorst, J. (1978). *Alexander, who used to be rich last Sunday.* New York: Atheneum.

Weiss, M.E. (1977). *Solomon Grundy, born on oneday: A finite arithmetic puzzle.* New York: Crowell.

White, E.B. (1942). *The trumpet of the swan.* New York: HarperCollins.

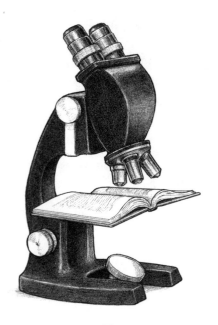

Chapter 5

Literature in the Science Program

Diane Lapp
James Flood

● ●

"**R**ead chapter four in your science book, answer the questions, and be ready for a quiz on this material." These familiar phrases echo in the ears of many adults and cause feelings of anxiety even though attending science classes may be years in the past. These feelings are also easily aroused when adults reencounter the end-of-the-chapter questions in science textbooks. Questions like "List at least three components of climate," "Explain how the way in which humans breathe is similar to and different from the way a fish breathes," and "What role do trees play in the water cycle?" can be intimidating and certainly don't help to convey the fascinating nature of scientific inquiry. Fortunately, when today's students are less than enthusiastic or even frightened about reading and studying their science textbooks, we ask why. A variety of causes and solutions present themselves.

Children often find themselves interested in scientific information when they encounter it in easy-to-read "literary" texts or trade books. The study of animals, for example, is common in the elementary classroom, and children are often enthusiastic about exploring this topic when it is introduced or developed through Eric Carle's *The Grouchy Ladybug* or *A House for Hermit Crab*. Similarly, much can be learned about the weather from David Wiesner's *Hurricane* and Verna Aardema's *Bringing the Rain to Kapiti Plain*; environmental issues are explored at an appropriate level for elementary school children in Michael J. Caduto and Joseph Bruchac's *Keepers of the Earth* and Aliki's *Corn Is Maize: The Gift of the Indians* (from HarperCollins's excellent Let's-Read-and-Find-Out series). But why do so many of our students experience difficulty with reading and maintaining interest in these topics when they appear in science textbooks?

Consider the following excerpts from fairly recent texts:

If it creeps, crawls, swims, flies, hops, or runs, it is probably a member of the animal kingdom. Animals are consumers; they can't make their own food. Animals, like plants, are many-celled, complex organisms. An animal cell has a nucleus and a nuclear membrane, but an animal cell doesn't have the rigid cell wall (Hackett & Moyer, 1991, p. 301, intended for sixth graders).

Water vapor in the air condenses in much the same way as water in your breath does. As warm air rises, it cools. As air cools, the water vapor in the air condenses into tiny droplets of water. The picture shows that many of these droplets come together to form clouds (Cohen et al., 1989, p. 231, intended for third graders).

Lead is a chemical given off when cars burn some kinds of fuel. Studies of ocean water, snow, and soil show that the air over the northern half of the earth has 1,000 times more lead than is natural. Newer cars have engines that use lead-free gasoline. As more and more older cars are replaced by newer cars, lead pollution might become less of a problem (Cohen et al., p. 279, intended for fifth graders).

These texts are not difficult if they are presented within an appropriate instructional context. While the authors of these and many other current science textbooks attempt to be sensitive to the demands of reading as well as to the relating of facts, content texts are not by nature predictable and are often conceptually dense. They frequently contain ideas that are completely unfamiliar to their readers, and these ideas are sometimes conveyed in difficult or technical terminology. The sixth grader who does not know the meaning of "nuclear membrane" or has no background knowledge of cells will not gain much from the first excerpt; the third grader who does not recognize "condenses" is likely to be baffled by the second excerpt. In addition, content text writers use exposition to present information; children are generally more familiar with narrative structure because it is common in the stories they hear or read. Finally, since explanations of many concepts must be condensed in science textbooks simply because of space considerations, the majority of texts do not provide adequate information for students to understand the nature of scientific phenomena or why they occur, to grasp the reasons that support scientific beliefs, or to be persuaded to pursue scientific investigations of their own.

In these days of scientific discovery and technological advances, abilities in science are increasingly important. Although the National Assessment of Educational Progress's *Science Report Card* (1988) notes that responses in the years since 1983 have indicated some progress, "average science proficiency across the grades remains distressingly low." These findings are of great concern to all educators involved in science instruction, and considerable research and inquiry is now being devoted to determining how to ensure increased science proficiency among students (Carlson, 1988).

One area receiving a great deal of attention is science textbooks. These lengthy expository texts are used to teach science about 90 percent of the time in American elementary school classrooms, and yet they are often introduced without adequate instruction for reading them (Harms, 1980; Yore, 1986). Reading instruction relies primarily on narrative texts, and it is rare if more than scant attention is paid to the different demands of reading exposition. Interestingly, National Assessment of Educational Progress data shows a decline in the reading scores of students in grades in which the primary reading material begins to shift from narration to exposition (Applebee,

Langer, & Mullis, 1988; Tierney & Lapp, 1979). This may occur because instruction in the reading of nonnarrative text does not accompany the shift in type of material being studied.

When teachers assign readings from science texts, they assume that the texts will provide students with information that they will be able to read and understand. For this assumption to be true, however, textbook authors must meet the following criteria:

1. Avoid depending on prior knowledge of the topic that readers may not have.
2. Use language that is not beyond the understanding of readers.
3. Use a text structure that is familiar to readers.
4. Present material in a manner that encourages readers to learn information.

Clearly these criteria are not always met. And when the language and knowledge base of the reader do not coincide with the science text, there is a likelihood of failure and a resulting loss of interest in science for that reader.

In part because of this increased attention to the difficulties many students have with reading science texts, many teachers today are attempting to develop instruction that will enable all students to use, expand, and transfer reading strategies needed to read and succeed with a wide variety of texts. Such instruction is based on the belief that (1) to read science texts successfully, students need to be able to observe, classify, predict, measure, and communicate; and (2) if students experience early success in science and in reading science texts, they will be motivated to continue studies in science. We believe that the use of literature as a complement to science textbooks can help students develop both the skills and the motivation to pursue scientific inquiry with enthusiasm and success.

Why Use Literature?

Our world is a complex place where events, issues, knowledge, feelings, and all the other things that make up existence resist being compartmentalized under headings such as science, social science, and the arts. School curricula that insist on a rigid distinction between areas of study do not serve to convey this sense of overlap. It is an awareness of this that encourages the continuing discussion among educators of an integrated curriculum, and it is in this spirit that we propose an integrated literature and science curriculum. Such a program can help students become familiar with language and text structure while introducing and expanding unfamiliar scientific terminology and concepts.

High-quality literature draws readers into the lives of the people it depicts. This feature, in turn, leads readers to make connections between their lives and the events related in books. One easy way to extend this connection into the realm of science is to encourage students to read biographies of people involved in scientific inquiry. Carole Briggs's *Women in Space: Reaching the Last Frontier*, Joan Dash's *The Triumph of Discovery: Women Scientists Who Won the Nobel Prize*, Jeri Ferris's *What Are You Figuring Now? A Story about Benjamin Banneker*, Russell Freedman's *The Wright Brothers: How They Invented the Airplane*, Jim Haskins's *Outward Dreams: Black Inventors and Their Inventions*, Johanna Hurwitz and Sue Hurwitz's *Sally Ride: Shooting for the Stars*, Stephanie McPherson's *Rooftop Astronomer: A Story about Maria Mitchell*, and Francene Sabin's *Elizabeth Blackwell: The First Woman Doctor* are just a few of the many fine science-related biographies available for young readers. Books such as these help students make a strong connection with science material, provide background knowledge and introduce new concepts and terms, and motivate readers to find out more.

Dole and Johnson (1981) suggest that fiction is another genre that can be used to motivate students and provide background for investigations in science; Guerra and Payne (1981) recommend using fiction as a primary source if the information presented is conceptually accurate. Smardo (1982) advocates integrating fiction and nonfiction in the science program by pointing out that while fiction cannot always clarify concepts, it can be part of the curriculum by providing the basis for a science lesson and further reading and by encouraging the development of reader interests. This balanced approach has literature serving as both a source of basic information and a motivating force.

Wide reading of good literature also improves reading and writing skills. Fox (1987, p. 23) points out that "reading one book teaches us how to read another. It's one of the 'prior knowledge' factors in reading." Practice with any type of reading benefits children's developing literacy abilities, and this practice is easier to encourage when texts are interesting and well written because from these texts "children [who are] struggling to learn to read find out that reading is worth the effort" (Cullinan, 1989, p. 137). Students' vocabularies increase and their comprehension skills develop as a result of reading a wide variety of books and stories. In addition, children who hear or read high-quality texts develop a sense of text structure, language, and content-specific information; they come to know what to expect from various types of texts and are able to predict what will happen next. This information enables them to better understand *all* the texts they read, including more difficult expository science texts.

With this talk of "skills" and "abilities," it is important to note that reading is no more a simple mastery of isolated skills than science is the mere memorization of facts and vocabulary. Rote memorization of scientific data does not necessarily increase knowledge or promote the ability to reason and see the relationships that are central in understanding scientific concepts. Reading involves the reader in an active process of "meaning making," as prior knowledge is linked with new information. Children must experience learning and build meaning for themselves; only then will they have learned to read—not decode—and to understand science concepts—not memorize them (Butzow & Butzow, 1989, p. xvii).

Starting Out with a Complementary Curriculum

When educators begin to explore the use of literature in the science curriculum, there are a number of issues they should keep in mind. First they must strive to ensure the integrity of both the science program and the reading program. Using literature and emphasizing reading in the science program is not intended to diminish the program's purpose—to teach about science—nor to eliminate the need for dedicated instruction in reading. Instead, the use of literature is meant to enhance science instruction by blending literary and scientific accounts of the same information. The following examples illustrate how such different accounts complement and reinforce learning on a single topic:

> Baby birds hatch from eggs. The parents usually protect and care for young birds. Notice how this bird feeds its young [illustrated by photographs]. The nest keeps the young birds warm (p. 32 of Cohen et al.'s *Discover Science* textbook, intended for grade 3).

Juan was full of curiosity about the swallows. He watched them build their small mud houses against the beams of the roof. The female sat quietly on her eggs while the male sang his twittering song to her. In the evening Juan saw them huddled close together, asleep (from Leo Politi's *Song of the Swallows*).

And on the subject of the environment:

Hunting laws do not allow people to hunt certain kinds of animals. Some laws limit the number of trees that can be cut down in forests. Other laws do not allow people to build houses, stores, or factories in certain places (p. 73 of Cohen et al.'s *Discover Science*, intended for grade 5).

Running Deer raced back to the village to tell everyone that the settlers were destroying the hunting grounds. The Indians knew that they must protect the land or their own food supply would be destroyed (from Thomas Locker's *The Land of Gray Wolf*).

And on fungi:

Look around the school grounds, a park, or a yard to find various kinds of fungi.... Obtain a field guide from the library to help you classify the fungi into groups. Observe the fungi again after one week. Record any changes you observe (p. 335 of Hackett & Moyer's *Science in Your World*, intended for grade 6).

The sun looked out from behind the clouds. And everyone came out from under the mushroom, bright and merry. The ant looked at his neighbors. "How could this be? At first I had hardly room enough under the mushroom just for myself, and in the end all five of us were able to sit under it" (from Mirra Ginsburg's *Mushroom in the Rain*).

These examples contrast just two of a possible variety of text formats that can be used to help students form a more complete basis for comprehension. For example, in addition to using a textbook passage and a trade book to explain how birds build nests and care for their young, an excerpt from a magazine (*Science World*, a magazine for elementary school readers, is a good choice) could be used as another source of information. Consider the additional data children would gain from reading the following passage:

Working like a basket maker, the male weaverbird builds his nest. He uses his beak to bend and interlace blades of grass and palm leaves. Nests are usually built on the ends of thin branches, with their "doorways" facing downward. The dangerous placement of the nest and its hard-to-find entrance provide protection from deadly tree snakes (Orlando, 1991).

When teachers are selecting literature to use in their science programs, they should keep in mind that its purpose is to enhance science learning. Using a variety of texts gives teachers flexibility and allows students to enter into a topic of study at their appropriate conceptual, language, and interest levels. Because narration is often easier than exposition for children to read, it naturally serves as an appropriate means of introducing students to many science topics. This does not mean, however, that literature can only be used in the early stages of investigating a new science topic. A broad range of texts—including textbook passages, poetry, magazine excerpts, storybooks, biography, narration, and science activity texts—used throughout the science program will benefit readers' understanding of concepts, improve literacy abilities, and keep motivation high. Use of a variety of texts also provides students with many models and ideas for their own oral and written literacy explorations. Literature may inspire these children to produce plays, conduct experiments, write songs, or share ideas.

There are, of course, many books available that could be used to complement basic science textbooks. The suggestions given in the figure on the next page are organized around topics commonly explored at the elementary level and could serve as a starting point.

The Program in Action

Once teachers determine that they want to use literature in their science programs, establish their instructional goals, and select a range of texts to share with their students, all that remains is the actual implementation of the curriculum. Different approaches work with different students, and teachers will quickly determine how to introduce and explore science topics in the best way in their own classrooms. Some students respond well to an initial read aloud and discussion of a storybook on a science topic, others

Books and Topics

Topic	Book	Comments
Animals	*Amazing Birds* (Alexandra Parsons)	lists different bird species
	Bear (John Schoenherr)	shows the bear in its natural habitat
	Birds Do the Strangest Things (Leonora and Arthur Hornblow)	describes bird behavior
	Dinosaur Dances (Jane Yolen)	poetry about children's favorite extinct species
	Egg to Chick (Millicent E. Selsam)	tells how birds reproduce
	Poems by Tony Johnston	includes a number of charming animal poems
	The Salamander Room (Anne Mazer)	tells readers what animals need
	Wings (Nick Bantock)	a pop-up book
Biology	*Biology for Every Kid* (Janice P. Van Cleave)	includes experiments to perform
Chemistry	*Chemistry for Every Kid* (Janice P. Van Cleave)	includes experiments to perform
Environment and the Earth	*Botany: Forty-Nine Science Fair Projects* (Dan Keen and Bob Bonnet)	full of good ideas
	Dinnertime (Jan Pienkowski)	a pop-up book good for beginning study of the food chain
	Janice Van Cleave's Earth Science for Every Kid (Janice P. Van Cleave)	includes experiments to perform
	Night and Day in the Desert (Jennifer Dewey)	describes this ecosystem
	Why the Tides Ebb and Flow (Joan Bowden)	retells an African folktale
Physics and Astronomy	*Astronomy* (Dennis B. Fradin)	a good source of general information
	Journey into a Black Hole (Franklyn M. Branley)	simplifies a complex topic
	Quillworker (Terri Cohlene)	retells a Cheyenne folktale
	Shooting Stars (Franklyn M. Branley)	explains a number of terms
	The Science Book of Light (Neil Ardley)	includes experiments to perform
	Uranus and *Jupiter* (Dennis B. Fradin)	introduce these planets

Lapp & Flood

prefer to read quietly and then gather in small groups to discuss their responses to a text, and still others may enjoy active involvement through an introductory experiment and demonstration.

As teachers discover for themselves the wide variety of possible texts and approaches available to them, they will develop or adapt their own unique style of teaching with literature in the science program. Some teachers, for example, use the often outstanding graphics, drawings, and photographs in trade books to supplement textbooks. Other teachers find that literature is useful in a number of highly specific ways including clarifying technical language, encouraging oral discussion of science topics, inspiring writing projects, and motivating students.

At the heart of the program, however, is the knowledge that an integrated approach has far-reaching benefits and is well worth the organizational effort to implement. When literature is part of the science program, both literacy learning and science learning are enhanced, and students are likely to become more enthusiastic about both the readingof science and scientific inquiry. In today's world, this is surely a goal worth striving for.

References

Applebee, A., Langer, J., & Mullis, I. (1988). *Who can read?* Princeton, NJ: Educational Testing Service.

Butzow, C., & Butzow, J. (1989). *Science through children's literature.* Englewood, CO: Libraries Unlimited.

Carlsen, W.S. (1988). *The effects of science teacher-subject matter knowledge on teacher questioning and classroom discourse.* Unpublished doctoral dissertation, Stanford University, Palo Alto, CA.

Cohen, M., Carney, T., Hawthorne, C., & McCormack, A. (1989). *Discover science.* Glenview, IL: Scott, Foresman.

Cullinan, B.E. (1989). *Literature and the child* (2nd ed.). Orlando, FL: Harcourt Brace Jovanovich.

Dole, J., & Johnson, V.R. (1981). Beyond the textbook: Science literature for young people. *Journal of Reading, 24,* 578-582.

Fox, M. (1987, January). The teacher disguised as writer, in hot pursuit of literacy. *Language Arts, 64,* 18-32.

Guerra, C.L., & Payne, D.B. (1981). Using popular books and magazines to interest students in general science. *Journal of Reading, 24,* 583-585.

Hackett, J.K., & Moyer, R.H. (1991). *Science in your world.* New York: Macmillan/McGraw Hill.

Harms, N. (1980). *Project synthesis: An interpretive consolidation of research identifying needs in natural science education* (Rep. NSF-SED-80-003). Washington, DC: National Science Foundation.

National Assessment of Educational Progress (1988). *Science report card.* Princeton, NJ: Educational Testing Service.

Smardo, F.A. (1982). Using children's literature to clarify science concepts in early childhood programs. *The Reading Teacher, 36,* 267-273.

Tierney, R.J., & Lapp, D. (1979). *National assessment of educational progress in reading.* Newark, DE: International Reading Association.

Yore, L.D. (1986, March). *What research says about science textbooks, science reading, and science reading instruction: A research agenda.* Paper presented at the annual meeting of the National Association for Research in Science Teaching, San Francisco, CA. (ED 269 243)

Children's Books

Aardema, V. (1981). *Bringing the rain to Kapiti Plain.* New York: Scholastic.

Aliki. (1976). *Corn is maize: The gift of the Indians.* New York: HarperCollins.

Ardley, N. (1991). *The science book of light.* Orlando, FL: Gulliver.

Bantock, N. (1991). *Wings: A pop-up book of things that fly.* New York: Random House.

Bowden, J. (1979). *Why the tides ebb and flow.* Boston, MA: Houghton Mifflin.

Branley, F.M. (1986). *Journey into a black hole.* New York: HarperCollins.

Branley, F.M. (1989). *Shooting stars.* New York: HarperCollins.

Briggs, C. (1988). *Women in space: Reaching the last frontier.* Minneapolis, MN: Lerner.

Caduto, M.J., & Bruchac, J. (1988). *Keepers of the earth: Native American stories and environmental activities for children.* Golden, CO: Fulcrum.

Carle, E. (1977). *The grouchy ladybug.* New York: Scholastic.

Carle, E. (1987). *A house for Hermit Crab.* New York: Scholastic.

Cohlene, T. (1990). *Quillworker: A Cheyenne legend.* Miami, FL: Rourke.

Dash, J. (1991). *The triumph of discovery: Women scientists who won the Nobel Prize.* Englewood Cliffs, NJ: Messner.

Dewey, J.O. (1991). *Night and day in the desert.* Boston, MA: Little, Brown.

Ferris, J. (1988). *What are you figuring now? A story about Benjamin Banneker.* Minneapolis, MN: Carolrhoda.

Fradin, D.B. (1983). *Astronomy.* Chicago, IL: Children's Press.

Fradin, D.B. (1989). *Jupiter.* Chicago, IL: Children's Press.

Fradin, D.B. (1989). *Uranus.* Chicago, IL: Children's Press.

Freedman, R. (1991). *The Wright brothers: How they invented the airplane.* New York: Holiday House.

Ginsburg, M. (1990). *Mushroom in the rain.* New York: Macmillan.

Haskins, J. (1991). *Outward dreams: Black inventors and their inventions.* New York: Walker.

Hornblow, L., & Hornblow, A. (1991). *Birds do the strangest things* (rev. ed.). New York: Random House.

Hurwitz, J., & Hurwitz, S. (1989). *Sally Ride: Shooting for the stars.* New York: Fawcett.

Johnston, T. (1990). *Poems by Tony Johnston.* New York: Putnam.

Keen, D., & Bonnet, B. (1989). *Botany: Forty-nine science fair projects.* Blue Ridge Summit, PA: TAB.

Locker, T. (1991). *The land of gray wolf.* New York: Dial.

Mazer, A. (1991). *The salamander room.* New York: Knopf.

McPherson, S. (1990). *Rooftop astronomer: A story about Maria Mitchell.* Minneapolis, MN: Carolrhoda.

Orlando, L. (1991, February 8). Decorating the den. *Science World,* 9-11.

Parsons, A. (1990). *Amazing birds.* New York: Knopf.

Pienkowski, J. (1981). *Dinnertime.* London: Gallery Five.

Politi, L. (1987). *Song of the swallows.* New York: Macmillan.

Sabin, F. (1982). *Elizabeth Blackwell: The first woman doctor.* Mahwah, NJ: Troll.

Schoenherr, J. (1991). *Bear.* New York: Philomel.

Selsam, M.E. (1987). *Egg to chick.* New York: HarperCollins.

Van Cleave, J.P. (1989). *Chemistry for every kid: 101 easy experiments that really work.* New York: Wiley.

Van Cleave, J.P. (1990). *Biology for every kid: 101 easy experiments that really work.* New York: Wiley.

Van Cleave, J.P. (1991). *Janice Van Cleave's earth science for every kid: 101 easy experiments that really work.* New York: Wiley.

Wiesner, D. (1990). *Hurricane.* New York: Clarion.

Yolen, J. (1990). *Dinosaur dances.* New York: Putnam.

Author Index

Children's Book Author Index

Waters, K., and M. Slovenz-Low, *Lion Dancer: Ernie Wan's Chinese New Year*, 24, 30
Weik, M.H., *The Jazz Man*, 26, 30
Weiss, M.E., *Solomon Grundy, Born on Oneday: A Finite Arithmetic Puzzle*, 63, 67
West, J.O., *Mexican-American Folklore*, 18, 30
White, E.B., *The Trumpet of the Swan*, 66, 67
White, F.M., *César Chávez: Man of Courage*, 20, 30
Wiesner, D., *Hurricane*, 69, 79
Williams, J. (*see* Ploski, H.A.)
Wilson, G. (*see* Moss, J.)
Wood, A.J., *Errata: A Book of Historical Errors*, 50, 56

Yarbrough, C., *Cornrows*, 23, 30
Yarbrough, C., *The Shimmershine Queens*, 26, 30
Yolen, J., *Dinosaur Dances*, 76, 79

Children's Book Title Index